D1233660

D

The Moral Dimension
of Marketing:
Essays on Business Ethics

The Moral Dimension of Marketing: Essays on Business Ethics

D. Kirk Davidson
Mount Saint Mary's College

AMERICAN MARKETING ASSOCIATION

Chicago, Illinois

© 2002 by D. Kirk Davidson
All rights reserved.

Library of Congress Cataloging-in-Publication Data

Davidson, D. Kirk.
   The moral dimension of marketing: essays on business ethics/D. Kirk Davidson.
      p. cm.
   Includes bibliographical references and index.
   ISBN 0-87757-300-X (alk. paper)
      1. Marketing—Moral and ethical aspects. 2. Marketing—Social aspects. 3. Business
   ethics. I. Title.

   HF5414 .D38 2002
   174′.4—dc21   2002074358

American Marketing Association
311 S. Wacker Dr., Suite 5800, Chicago, Illinois 60606 USA
Francesca Van Gorp Cooley, Director of Publications
Charles Chandler, Editorial Project Assistant
Mary Loye, Design and Compositor

Cover design by Liz Novak.
Cover photo: Martin Barraud/Stone/Getty One

No part of this publication may be reproduced, stored in a retrieval system, transmitted,
or utilized in any form or by any means, including electronic, mechanical, photocopy-
ing, recording, or otherwise, without the written permission of the American Marketing
Association.

Printed in the United States of America

An author is indeed blessed if he has a good editor—in which case I am doubly blessed because I am married to one. Sandra, you have been a part and a supporter of this book from its inception. This collection of essays has benefited enormously from your sensitive and professional work and the always-respectful use of your red pen. For the many hours you spent poring over this manuscript—and for the countless other blessings you have brought to my life—I am deeply grateful.

About the Author

D. Kirk Davidson has spent his entire life in and around marketing. Born to a family of merchants in the Midwest, he earned his BA from Princeton and his MBA from Harvard. He then spent 12 years with RH Macy in a variety of marketing and management positions, and for the next 20 years, he served as chief executive officer of Mark Fenwick, Inc., a group of women's apparel stores in California. In midlife, he switched his career to academia, earned a Ph.D. from Golden Gate University, and for 11 years has taught business ethics and marketing courses at Mount Saint Mary's College, where he is an associate professor and department chair. He is currently preparing the second edition of his book, *Selling Sin: The Marketing of Socially Unacceptable Products*.

Table of Contents

Acknowledgments

I would like to acknowledge three men—all friends and valued colleagues—who unknowingly contributed to this book in that they influenced the development of my thinking about moral behavior in the interaction between buyers and sellers. **Thomas Berry** has the most extraordinary intellect I have ever known. It is through him—in several memorable dinner conversations at his retreat overlooking the Hudson River—that I first became aware of the need for human systems, including marketing, to conform to and be an integral part of the cosmos and its governing systems. It was **Kirk Hanson** who first introduced me to the challenges and excitement of the business and society and business ethics fields of study. Twenty years ago, he generously invited me to participate in his classes at Stanford Business School, shared case studies with me, and encouraged me to become an active scholar in these disciplines. One name, **Ralph Nader**, stands alone as the consummate defender of consumer rights and interests. He has devoted a lifetime of passionate, tireless, and innovative work and insisted that marketers offer safe products, price them fairly, and advertise them honestly. All consumers owe him a debt of gratitude for his advocacy on their behalf, and I thank him for providing the inspiration for my work.

Men are qualified for civil liberty in exact proportion to their disposition to put moral chains upon their own appetites. Society cannot exist unless a controlling power on will and appetite be placed somewhere, and the less of it there is within, the more there must be without. It is ordained in the eternal order of things that men of intemperate minds cannot be free. Their passions forge their fetters.

—*Edmund Burke, 1729–1797*

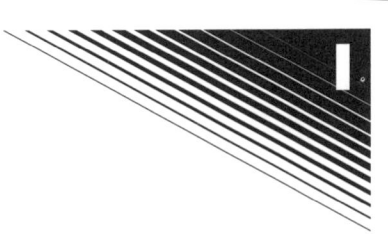

OVERVIEW

W hat a strange and difficult problem we face in talking or writing about the subject of morality in marketing or business ethics. For at least three thousand years, religious teachers and philosophers have offered warnings and proscriptions. There is a substantial body of literature on the subject from academics and business managers alike. It is common for chief executive officers of major corporations to make public statements that embrace the concept, yet we still hear with surprising frequency, "Isn't business ethics an oxymoron?"

This question would never have gained such widespread notoriety if there were not at least some truth to it and if there were not a serious issue embedded in a rather glib exterior. There is indeed some element of tension or conflict between the practice of business management and what we normally think of as ethical, or moral, behavior. Were this not so, the discipline of business ethics would never have blossomed into such an interesting, challenging, and important field of study.

If the connection between the general practice of business management and ethical behavior is difficult for some marketers to comprehend, how much more challenging it must be to contemplate such a thing as "marketing ethics." Imagine the typical marketing executive. Along with the usual characteristics we might hope to find in any business manager—the ability to think clearly, solve problems, manage people well, and create and implement rational plans—we also hope that the marketer is gregarious, entrepreneurial, and perhaps even a bit aggressive, fast thinking, fast acting, and fast talking. Thus, trying to link ethical behavior with marketing, establish some ethical boundaries for marketing activities, and search for ways to be effective marketers and salespeople while adhering to generally accepted ethical practices might appear to be a particularly wild goose chase.

But, however wild the chase, it is an important one to pursue. Marketing, in its broadest sense, is at the very core of all business activity. Therefore, if we are to gain an understanding of what constitutes ethical behavior in the general conduct of business activities, we must not ignore the more specific concerns and questions as to what constitutes proper behavior in the practice of marketing.

To study ethics is to study tension: tension between right and wrong, good and bad; between acceptable and unacceptable behavior; and between competing paradigms. If there are not at least two perspectives with some degree of difference between them, there can be no concept of ethics. To think of or talk about ethical behavior, we need some opposing idea or action with which to compare or contrast it.

In business, and especially in the function of marketing, there is no shortage of tension. Every business transaction involves a buyer and a seller, and these two parties will have divergent interests that create an element of tension. The current fascination with "relationship marketing" notwithstanding, each party to a sale or marketing agreement must and will be looking out for its own interests. This tension is especially important in consumer goods marketing, as opposed to business-to-business marketing. In consumer goods marketing, the balance, or rather the imbalance, of power between the two parties is all the more problematic. It is here that we come face to face with the stark question: Is marketing, at its most fundamental, a cooperative or an adversarial relationship?

Semantics

As is already apparent, the words "ethical" and "moral" have been used interchangeably. Although this may be unsettling for some readers, the meanings are close enough for the purposes of this book.

The terms "business ethics" and "marketing ethics" both enjoy widespread usage, but they also pose certain problems of semantics. Although there might be general agreement that a seller withholding important information from a buyer is *immoral*, how do we determine what is *moral*? It is easier to characterize actions as immoral than to define moral activity, and the terms acquire something of a negative bias. In the same vein, there are many marketing issues that do not fit easily within the terms "moral" or "immoral." For example, we might praise a firm that contributes 5% of its profits to charitable causes, but we probably would not characterize this as moral behavior, and we certainly would not label a firm that contributes only 2% of its profits as immoral.

For reasons of semantics, then, I use the more inclusive phrase "social issues in marketing" rather than more limiting phrases such as "marketing ethics" or "marketing morality." This book takes as its subject the overall impact of marketing on society. It encompasses the broad range of interaction between an organization's marketing function, in its most comprehensive definition, and a wide variety of business and nonbusiness groups and individuals. Our first challenge is to examine how an organization's marketing activities affect its customers, because the relationship between an organization and its customers is arguably the most important. We also want to examine the impact of the organization on all levels and varieties of government agencies, communities, advocacy groups, the media, suppliers, and so on. Then we must ask what are the proper, the acceptable, the just, and, yes, the "moral" parameters of those interactions.

This broader, more inclusive terminology becomes all the more important as we read and hear increasingly about such areas as cause-related marketing and strategic philanthropy. The connection between these subjects and the broad field of social issues in marketing has yet to be fully explored.

Common Material

As a more focused category, marketing ethics shares many concepts and tools with its parent discipline, business ethics. For example, every business ethics text offers two fundamental ways of analyzing ethical dilemmas: what is usually referred to as a utilitarian approach and a principle-based (or deontological) approach. The former asks us to consider which of the available courses of action will result in "the greatest good for the greatest number;" in other words, which choice will create the greatest net benefit for the entire society. The latter requires us to adhere in our actions and decisions to certain universally admired standards of conduct—for example, honesty, loyalty, integrity, fairness, beneficence—without regard for the outcomes. These tools of the business ethics trade apply equally well to ethical dilemmas encountered in the marketing function.

Business ethics teaches about the importance of values as marketers go about the decision-making process. Awareness or adoption of certain values and their application will be influenced by various personal factors (e.g., demographic information, family circumstances, training and education) as well as by external or social forces (e.g., organizational pressures, emulation of certain friends or social groups). Again, these concepts are just as appropriate and important in the study of marketing ethics as in the study of the broader area of business ethics.

Organization of the Book

The four P's of marketing—product, price, promotion, and place (or distribution)—are still a standard feature of every marketing textbook. Although they may seem a bit trite after many decades of use, they are hard to ignore. Therefore, many of the essays in this book have been organized loosely around the four P's, with a group of essays devoted to each. Although there are many issues of proper or ethical behavior and acceptable marketing practices related to each of these four elements of the marketing mix, there are also serious questions related to the subject of targeting, and therefore a section is devoted to targeting. In addition, because there is so much interest and concern of late surrounding questions of privacy, there is a section on that subject. Finally, a group of essays is also included under the heading "Inappropriate Marketing." These essays pertain to important issues that do not fit easily under moral or ethical descriptions.

Following each essay are two or three questions that deal with the most important issues or problems in that essay. Students may find these questions useful in stimulating and focusing their thinking about the essay. Professors may want to ask their students to answer these questions either in writing or verbally, or they may simply choose to use these questions as starting points for class discussions.

Subjective Material

Because this is a collection of essays and not a textbook, I have made no attempt to hide my personal perspective on the issues. The essays are unabashedly subjective. It is expected that there can and will be other points of view expressed by marketers, students, and other professors. As in all problems of ethics, answers or solutions that can satisfy all challenges are notoriously difficult to find. Different points of view should lead to lively discussion and debate, the most effective way of learning about complex issues.

Make no doubt about it, these *are* complex issues. There are always two or more sides to all of the issues addressed in this collection. There are never easy or definitive answers; if there were, the issues or problems would not be worth addressing. The lack of answers is often frustrating to students and professors alike, not to mention to the marketing executives faced with making a decision when there are at best only obscure guidelines to follow. There is general agreement that it is too late to try to teach ethical behavior at the college and postgraduate levels. But what we can do—and what this book strives to do—is to make marketers and soon-to-be marketers aware of the moral dimensions that accompany so many of their decisions and to stimulate thoughtful discussion around those moral dimensions. Although this effort falls short of finding "answers," it is reasonable to expect that such awareness will in itself lead to a higher level of ethical behavior and to a more consistent and sensitive understanding of marketing's impact on so many segments of society.

This would be no small achievement. In my years of learning and teaching about social issues in marketing, I have reached two firm conclusions. First, if the actions of marketers and other business managers do not meet the expectations of the society in which they operate, a gap is created that will not go long unfilled. Of necessity, something will move in to fill that gap and force those unacceptable marketing practices more in line with society's expectations. That "something" may be government action (e.g., new laws, new regulations), pressure from advocacy groups, or changes initiated by the marketing organizations themselves. Therefore, foresighted marketers do have some control over their environment.

Second, there is tension—sometimes conflict—between *economic* goals and *ethical* goals. To reach one or the other of these goals is no small feat, but it is certainly not unusual. That is, it is not so difficult for a marketer to run a profitable operation if ethical or social issues can be ignored. Likewise, it is relatively easy for a marketer to stay within the bounds of ethics and acceptable social standards if making a profit was not essential. The great challenge for practitioners, teachers, and students is to accomplish these goals simultaneously: to operate economically *and* efficiently, to build market share and establish brand names and a good customer base *and* behave ethically, and to make a satisfactory profit *and* still contribute to the well-being of society overall. Reaching these goals is a challenge worthy of our best efforts, and the purpose of this book is to contribute to that end.

1

Does Marketing Have a Place in Utopia?

There is no shortage of social and economic troubles in the United States. Some business critics claim that marketing contributes to these troubles. Throughout the history of Western culture, the marketing function has been suspect at best, if not detested. In the writings of all three major Abrahamic religions—Christianity, Judaism, and Islam—there are moral questions about the dealings between buyers and sellers. In contrast, business supporters and apologists argue that marketing brings about improvements in social and economic conditions. The ongoing dialogue between these "voices" is an important part of marketing ethics.

It was with special interest, therefore, that I read a 1996 article from the *Journal of Marketing Management* titled, "Marcadia Postponed: Marketing, Utopia, and the Millennium." Written by three scholars from Northern Ireland—Stephen Brown, Pauline Maclaren, and Lorna Stevens—the article explores the relationship of marketing to our mythological and cultural views of the concept of utopia. Marketing is criticized because it encourages consumer desire, frivolity, and unwanted expenditures and capitalizes on greed, selfishness, pride, and sloth. There is plenty of material for an essay on morality in marketing. But marketing is also about creating utopias. "Marketing is arguably the keeper of the ... utopian flame" (Brown, Maclaren, and Stevens 1996, p. 676).

Let's test these conflicting views by considering three icons of present-day marketing in the United States: Disneyland, McDonald's, and Wal-Mart. There are plenty of voices to argue the many reasons these institutions are the antithesis of a utopia. Disneyland is by definition a fantasy: unreal, unnatural, a mere plastic cartoon imitation of our dreams. McDonald's, nutritional concerns aside, is the ultimate in mass production and mass consumption. The brand name has even acquired a dubious distinction: Its first two letters "Mc" now connote a pejorative description of boring standardization, a lack of interest, and a total absence of sophistication. The authors note (p. 675) that, from a consumer standpoint, "the McDonald's experience—McTopia—has been depicted in grotesque, nightmarish terms." And Wal-Mart? Would it not be more likely to hear a Wal-Mart store described as a wasteland than as a utopia, with aisle after dreary aisle of shower curtains and electric-toaster boxes stacked high and rack after rack of sweatshirts and ersatz "designer" jeans?

There is another, quite different point of view, however, that is less jaded, less cynical, and less elitist. Here, Disneyland is wholesome entertainment—good, clean, family fun and a wonderful way to escape from the humdrum and stress of our daily lives. Our dreams come true and our fantasies come to life right before our eyes, if only for a few magical hours. Is that such a bad description of utopia?

At McDonald's, we always know what we are going to get, whether in Moscow, Idaho, or in Moscow, Russia. The menu is the same with some minor variations to please local palates. The food is prepared in the same way and tastes exactly as we expect, the surroundings are clean, and the values are honest. Is there a child, or even an adult, who comes away from McDonald's dissatisfied? What other institution can claim such a consistent batting average in bringing a bit of joy and relaxation into our lives? That should qualify as some sort of modern-day utopia.

Wal-Mart, with its Arkansas roots and small-town beginnings in the cities that more sophisticated merchants ignored, never pretended to be fancy, never tried to put on airs, and never wavered from its appeal to middle-income America. The firm has relentlessly searched for and found new ways to drive down the cost of distribution and pass those savings on to its customers. Its success is measured not only in its unchallenged role as the largest and most formidable retailer in the world, but also in its raising the standard of living and bringing true savings to millions of consumers. Is that not a utopian ideal?

The article by Brown, Maclaren, and Stevens was written with an eye toward the twenty-first century. It led me to question and formulate some thoughts on the future of the marketing profession. I believe society's love/hate relationship with marketing will continue. Marketers will go on demonstrating some less-than-admirable qualities such as greed and selfishness. Because the marketing psyche is naturally competitive and aggressive, excessive and unethical behavior will persist. However, marketing will still be the indispensable link between production and consumption. Marketing will continue to aid in bringing a higher standard of living to more of the world's population. And through what is now known as social marketing, an ever-widening array of public policy programs is being pursued through tried-and-true concepts of marketing.

In the future, a positive and hopeful aspect of marketing will develop: a heightened awareness of its moral dimension. The fields of business ethics and business and society, as serious areas of study for both academics and managers, are barely 30 years old. The narrower fields of marketing ethics and social issues in marketing are younger still. Marketers will be more reflective about what they do as a result of these relatively new fields. They will be more conscious of marketing's effects, good and bad, on their businesses and on the greater society in which their businesses operate. I believe that this heightened awareness, though it will not correct all the excesses and mistakes that philosophers and theologians have cataloged for so many years, nevertheless will lead to a higher and more consistent level of ethical and socially conscious marketing decisions.

As this new century—this new millennium—gets underway, it may no longer be in vogue to search for a utopia. But marketers have the opportunity and the obligation to focus on the true bottom line of their profession: to maintain the legitimacy of marketing. To do this, they must add value not only to the coffers of their respective companies, but also to the well-being of the broader society. Heretofore, marketing and society have had a respect/revile relationship, but marketers have it within their power to tip the scale toward respect.

1. Why should marketing be respected? Why should it be reviled?

2. Consider another marketing powerhouse in recent decades: Nike. Has Nike contributed to some social problems, or has it been part of a solution?

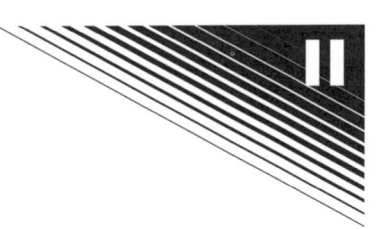

TARGETING

Introduction

The purpose of this section is to wrestle with the question: Is there anything unethical about targeting? Today, targeting is very much in the mainstream of marketing theory and practice; it is an essential component of any sound marketing strategy. Every marketing textbook will explain that the mass market can be segmented in several ways—geographic, demographic, and so on—and that the wise marketer will then target the segments that hold the most promise and the most profit. Only then can a marketer devise an effective and efficient strategy that will result in a product that is designed, packaged, priced, promoted, and distributed specifically for the targeted group of customers.

So far, so good. No moral problems yet, because we are making the assumption that buyers and sellers come together with nearly equal standing in the market. But what if their standing is *not* equal? What if the buyers fall into a category deemed for one reason or another vulnerable? Children, for example. Sometimes senior citizens, sometimes women, sometimes various ethnic groups. Now there is a question of fairness; now there is a problem of ethics.

Is it fair, for example, if marketers target children, using all the highly developed and highly persuasive tactics that Madison Avenue advertising professionals can bring to bear on this segment of the market? In general, children are less experienced, less sophisticated, and certainly less mature than adults. They are less competent to make informed decisions about what they see advertised on television and what they see on the shelves of supermarkets. For years, concerns have been focused on the propriety of advertising sugar-coated cereal products on Saturday morning cartoon programs, where the lines are blurred between the advertising messages and the cartoon content because the same animated characters are used. Likewise, we cry foul when movie studios and record labels promote violent or explicitly sexual films and compact discs in magazines read by teens and preteens.

When marketers of home security devices target senior citizens using high-pressure tactics that exploit unreasonable fear, society believes that is not fair. When manufacturers of malt liquors with high alcoholic content target young, low-income African American males, critics say that is not fair. When cigarette manufacturers target young women with only limited education, society says that is not fair.

How, then, to make sense of all this? What is fair, and what is not? Despite its negative connotations, targeting is a perfectly acceptable marketing tactic. Even targeting children, ethnic groups, or other so-called vulnerable segments is not in and of itself unfair. For example, there is nothing objectionable about personal-care manufacturers designing hair care products specifically for Asian Americans or African Americans and promoting those products directly to those markets. However, the three-way combination of targeting, vulnerable segments, *and* a product that has some health or welfare risk—for example, cigarettes, alcoholic beverages, and even sugar-coated cereals—is sure to set off societal warning signals.

Like so many marketing tactics, targeting must be used with sensitivity and restraint. It is a powerful, necessary part of the marketer's bag of tools, but it can cause harm. When the buyer does not have the ability to make informed decisions because of, for example, a lack of knowledge, maturity, or judgment, the seller has an unfair advantage. Under these circumstances, marketing ceases to be a cooperative relationship and becomes adversarial. A gap is created between organizational performance (the unfair targeting) and societal expectations. The question then becomes, How will that gap be filled? Will the marketer exercise restraint? Will advocacy groups or consumers' cooperative organizations come along to strengthen the buyers' standing in the marketplace with increased knowledge about the product? Will the government—federal, state, or local—step in with legislation and regulations to protect the vulnerable, adding yet another bureaucratic burden onto the business community?

These are some of the ethical concerns surrounding the practice of targeting. Although there are certainly lessons to be learned from the following examples, marketers still must weigh the moral consequences of their actions with each new situation, each new product, or each new target. Profitability *and fairness* are the twin goals marketers must pursue.

Targeting Minorities

2

By now, it is common knowledge that the population of the United States is becoming increasingly diverse. Groups that we have thought of as minorities will in the aggregate make up a majority of the population within a few years. African Americans, Latinos, Asian Americans, and other ethnic groups are growing faster than the Caucasian segment of the population.

Marketers are keenly aware of these changing demographics. It is their business, after all, to respond to the shifting social environment; to segment the overall market into smaller, more homogeneous groups, often along ethnic lines; and to understand as much as possible the different behavioral patterns of their potential customers in each of those groups. Products are designed or redesigned for these individual segments. Advertising messages are written specifically to appeal to these segments; for example, ads are often in Spanish and aired on Spanish-language radio and television stations.

For the astute marketer, these changes represent a considerable opportunity, but they pose challenges as well. The U.S. society not only condones but also expects marketers to recognize the importance of these ethnic segments by creating new or redesigned products and by delivering advertising messages in languages other than English when it is appropriate. But society will not tolerate exploitation, or even perceived exploitation, of these groups. Two examples come to mind from the recent past, and both happen to involve the targeting of African Americans.

The first example involves the marketing of cigarettes. In 1990, R.J. Reynolds Tobacco Co. test-marketed a new brand of cigarettes called Uptown. Reynolds had learned from its marketing research that African Americans were likely to prefer menthol flavored cigarettes, and the company reasoned that it could do well with a cigarette brand that specifically targets this group. So it formulated Uptown with a strong menthol taste, chose a package with colors and graphics that scored well among Blacks in focus groups, and even designed the package to be opened in a manner familiar to many African Americans. Reynolds chose Philadelphia as its test market because of its large African American population. It created magazine and billboard ads using African American models. In short, Reynolds put together a classic textbook marketing strategy.

Contrary to the textbooks, however, the market test was an unmitigated disaster. Criticism poured in from federal health officials, anti-tobacco advocates, and community leaders. The basis of the criticism was that it was unfair and absolutely unethical for the company to target a group that already suffers from more than its share of health problems with a product that causes much harm and death.

Caught off-guard, Reynolds responded that African Americans, similar to Caucasians, should be able to choose for themselves whether to smoke and should have the option to choose a cigarette produced to their liking. But the steady barrage of criticism was unrelenting, and Reynolds finally scrapped the Uptown project to avoid further negative publicity. Lost in the swirl of inflammatory debate was the fact that the new product had enjoyed considerable, albeit brief, success with its targeted market.

The second example involves the marketing of alcohol. Several brewers, both large and small, include malt liquors in their product lines. Malt liquors are beverages that are similar to beer but have a 20%–30% higher alcoholic content and carry brand names such as Colt 45, Midnight Dragon, and PowerMaster. The brewers know from their marketing research that young, inner-city African American males are a major market for malt liquors.

Therefore, it made sense for brewers to promote these beverages in urban Black neighborhoods using media and content that would appeal to this target market: "gangsta" rap music on Black radio stations and point-of-purchase displays featuring sexy, young Black women. Again, it was a textbook approach to putting together a successful marketing strategy. And, again, there was an explosion of outrage from many social groups: community activists, health officials, and anti-alcohol advocates. The manufacturers were roundly criticized for targeting a segment of the population that was already troubled with a higher-than-average incidence of alcohol-related health problems with a potent brew often sold in 40-ounce bottles. This strategy, critics claimed, was certain to result in more alcohol addiction, abuse of women, property destruction, and all the other predictable inner-city crimes.

The cigarette and brewers were quick to respond to their critics with the argument that it is patronizing and condescending for society to object to these targeted marketing campaigns. They claimed that the critics' unspoken assumption was that African Americans, or whatever the targeted minority happens to be, are less able than others to make good choices about their buying habits and their health. The marketers behind these campaigns pointed out that their products are legal and are intended for adult customers, and neither the marketers nor society in general should decide that certain racial or ethnic groups need protection. There is validity to this view, but it is an intellectual argument that is unlikely to carry much weight in the arena of public opinion.

Marketers are left with two lessons. First, although the concept of targeting may be innocent enough, the targeting of potentially harmful products to groups that a society might consider vulnerable is fraught with potential problems. Such targeting is certain to attract the attention and the wrath of consumer advocacy groups that will take advantage of their ability to drum up exposure in the media. The result is sure to be an unrelenting, unpleasant, and unprofitable public relations battle for the company.

Second, emotion will win over political or philosophical reasoning. Advocates and community activists can mount a very persuasive charge of unethical practices against the marketers' claims to free speech or concerns about patronizing behavior. Marketers' past sins, or at least their lack of restraint, will come back to haunt them. The public will be only too willing to believe that marketers are again attempting to exploit a disadvantaged or vulnerable group.

1. If it is acceptable for companies to create certain products—for example, hair care products—for specific racial or ethnic groups, do you believe it is wrong for alcohol or cigarette manufacturers to create products for these same groups?

2. In the U.S. society, who decides which segments of the population are vulnerable and deserve a greater level of protection from marketers?

3

Targeting Children

The place: Disney's Yacht and Beach Resort in Orlando, Fla. The attraction: an event titled Kid Power. Hundreds flocked to the conference. Yet these were not children crowding through the doors but adults, serious marketing professionals bent on learning more about how to market their wares to children more effectively and efficiently.

On the program was a veritable who's who of children's marketing firms: Lego, Nickelodeon, Hasbro, Club Disney, and Chuck E. Cheese. The various segments of the entertainment industry were also well represented: Sony Wonder, Time Inc. Kids, Universal Studios, and so on. Even Nissan gave a presentation.

It will come as no surprise that these annual three-day conferences draw big crowds—even at $1,300–$1,700 per person for the registration, plus travel, meals, and lodging. Marketing to kids is big business, and it is getting bigger. Recently, *BusinessWeek* magazine estimated that, with allowances, earnings, and gifts, children 14 years of age and younger accounted for $20 billion of direct spending annually and that they influenced another $200 billion in consumer purchases. The children of the now-middle-aged baby boomers recently became the largest children's segment in history, surpassing even their parents. What self-respecting marketer of any product or service even remotely associated with children would not want to tap into this growing, impressionable, and lucrative audience?

In a previous time, marketers would have aimed their messages at the children's parents, who made the buying decisions and actual purchases, but such is no longer the case in many product categories. Now the messages are likely to be beamed directly at children. As one candid advertising agency executive stated, "We're relying on the kid to pester the mom to buy the product."

However, from a marketing ethics perspective, the dangers are clear enough: Children are the quintessential "vulnerable" target market. They are inexperienced, unsophisticated, and, of course, less mature than adults. So they can hardly be expected to have equal standing when they come into the marketplace to spend their allowance and gift money and are confronted by billion dollar corporations and their Madison Avenue agents.

Furthermore, nothing is as likely to enrage parents, and society in general, as the prospect of marketers manipulating and taking advantage of children to pad their profits. Consider the following:

◆In 1998, Congress was on track to pass comprehensive tobacco regulation as long as the national debate remained focused on the 3000 teenagers who become addicted to tobacco every day. The bill included all manner of protections aimed at children: no billboard advertising of tobacco products near schools, serious restrictions on cigarette advertising in publications with significant teenage readership, further restrictions on point-of-purchase display advertising in retail stores, and so on. The proposed marketing regulations failed only after the tobacco industry, with a massive $40 million advertising blitz, shifted the focus of the issue away from children and onto the tax-and-spend tendencies of Congress.

◆In recent years, the most controversial characters in beer advertising have been the Budweiser frogs and lizards and Bud Light's *bon-vivant* dog Spuds McKenzie because, it is claimed, these icons appeal to children. For the same reason, shifting back to the tobacco industry, Joe Camel and the Marlboro Man have both been highly criticized on the grounds that they are meant to appeal to children.

◆There is ongoing controversy about marketing in schools. In a Faustian bargain, some schools receive badly needed television equipment, and in exchange, Channel One brings its requisite dose of advertising right into the classroom during each hour of educational programming. A school principal may be asked to hand out coupons for JCPenney's jeans to go along with the Channel One commercials and to round out the promotion strategy for the product. The cafeteria may feature fast food from Taco Bell, Arby's, or Pizza Hut with the requisite brand identification.

◆In the central lobby of my grandson's middle school, there are two large lighted displays. One features an ad for Reese's candy bars, despite parents' and school officials' concerns that the students are eating too much sugar. The other is for Nintendo's Gamecube, and it promises "comic mischief" and "mild violence."

◆Now there is the Internet. "As millions of kids go online, marketers are in hot pursuit," Sandberg (1997) warned a few years ago in *The Wall Street Journal*. Companies offer children an enticing array of games and contests, but to receive this feast of entertainment, youngsters must fill out questionnaires about themselves, their families, and their friends—information the companies add to their databases for future use.

Marketers must remember that along with the bright opportunities to advertise and sell to millions of children with increasing purchasing power, there is a serious threat as well. Push too hard or manipulate too aggressively and society will turn on the marketer with a vengeance.

Boycotts, angry letters, op-ed pieces, bad public relations, and even picketing at board of directors' meetings, not to mention restrictive legislation and regulation at the state and federal levels, are all part of the arsenal available to parents who are motivated to protect their children from the harms, perceived or real, threatened by overly ambitious marketers.

In every business ethics class, it is almost certain that at some point, someone will ask the question, "Where do we draw the line?" Every firm should wrestle with this question when it plans a strategy of targeting and marketing to children. Of course, marketers want to tell children about their new products: where to buy them, how much they cost, how they work, and all the other essentials of marketing. This informational aspect of advertising will normally be welcomed. It is the persuasive aspect of advertising to children and other vulnerable groups that is most suspect, and that is where marketers must draw the hypothetical line. Parents and their consumer advocate partners will not tolerate marketers that focus their high-powered, high-tech Madison Avenue advertising tactics on their children.

Again, there must be a balance between economics and ethics. Marketers must beware of going too far over the line, of emphasizing economics and giving short shrift to ethics. That large market of gullible children may look like a marketer's dream come true. But a public backlash, brought on by perceived exploitation of children, may turn the dream into every marketer's worst nightmare.

1. What special ethical concerns do marketers face in marketing their products to children?

2. Should public schools be advertising-free zones? Why, or why not?

4

Targeting the Mentally Disabled

Marketers are all too aware, or should be, of the ethical problems and risks posed by marketing to so-called vulnerable groups. Various advocacy organizations have complained for years about how producers of breakfast cereals and toys target young children with Saturday morning, cartoon-related advertising. Others have exposed the ethical hazards of marketing to the elderly. Manufacturers of cigarettes and alcoholic beverages have incited their critics when they have targeted women and minorities.

Thus, I read with considerable dismay the following headline from an issue of *The Wall Street Journal*: "Credit Cards Invade a New Market Niche: The Mentally Disabled" (Cahill 1998). Many commentators have argued at length that women and minorities should not be considered vulnerable; some have even pushed the case further to state that children are fair game for aggressive marketers. But would anyone deny that the mentally disabled should be spared or protected from the hardball tactics of modern day marketing?

Of late, increasing numbers of the mentally disabled are living independently. They manage their lives reasonably well, often with considerable help from family members and friends. Some rely solely on welfare, and others hold part-time jobs. But this trend comes at precisely the same time that competition among credit card marketers has reached new heights. Saturation mailings have become the marketing tool of choice in this industry: Several billion applications are sent out each year, as most of us know well enough from the familiar solicitation letters we receive on a weekly basis. This combination of social and competitive market forces creates a real dilemma. Commenting on the credit card industry's growing hunger for new customers, Cahill (1998, p. A1) states that "there is an inevitable collision between the sharp-elbowed world of consumer credit and some of society's most trusting and vulnerable citizens."

21

As with so many ethical problems, it is easy enough to frame the issue, but it is difficult to find a satisfactory answer. No one is suggesting that the mentally disabled, as a group, should be denied credit. Indeed, such discrimination in lending practices would be illegal in some states. Because there is no clear definition of mental disability, there is no confidence about where to draw the line between those who are able to manage credit and those who are not. How could a credit card issuer ascertain that an applicant is mentally disadvantaged from the information received through the mail or even over the telephone? Face-to-face issuing of credit is a thing of the past.

Common sense would be a good place to start, however. A mentally disabled man in Newton, Iowa, lives on his own and has a part-time job mopping floors at a fast-food restaurant. The telephone solicitor who "sold" the man on accepting a Visa credit card from a Maryland bank noted his place of employment correctly, but entered his annual income as $70,000.

Issuing the plastic cards is only the beginning of the problem, of course. Managing the credit is another matter. If a credit card holder makes the necessary minimum payments over even a brief period of time, it is likely that the maximum allowed credit will be bumped up when the holder approaches it. This is part of card issuers' marketing strategy, and it may even be programmed into their computers. The average person gives in to the temptation of "maxxing out" his or her credit card easily enough. A mentally disabled cardholder is all the more likely to succumb to the blandishments of pervasive telephone and television sales pitches. Cahill (1998) tells of one such man who purchased eight credit card protection plans, dental insurance, renter's insurance, legal insurance, life insurance, and, even though he did not have a driver's license, a roadside-assistance plan. What happens when this unsophisticated cardholder gets so deeply into debt that, on the basis of his modest income, there is no hope of extricating himself? Should the card issuer or the store go after his personal assets, if he has any? Or perhaps go after his family's assets to save him the embarrassment of a bankruptcy?

There is a wrong being done here, but there is no clear course toward making it right, and there is even less clarity regarding how to prevent it in the first place. In a simpler age, a local banker knew the person who sat across the desk and applied for credit and could judge the person's abilities and potential. A store owner or manager could make a conscious decision over the counter, regarding a customer's credit limit.

If buyers are to benefit fully from the marvels of technology—of computers and automated telephone marketing systems, of total-convenience purchasing through catalogs, the telephone, and the Internet—so that they no longer come face-to-face with the seller, then the social problems that inevitably come in the wake of such advances must be solved. Almost every day, technological problems that push high-tech marketing to new limits are solved. Although we glory in these large benefits, let us not forget the small burdens and problems that are created in the process.

In the classic buyer–seller transaction, the responsibility for a mutually satisfactory outcome is borne equally by the two parties. If the buyer is disabled, however, the responsibility shifts heavily to the seller. Sellers and issuers of credit, therefore, must be willing to bear the costs associated with that responsibility—writing off the bad debts run up by the mentally disadvantaged more quickly and being more judicious in the issuance of credit cards. They must factor in these costs when they decide whether to adopt the hard-sell, high-tech marketing techniques that are becoming increasingly prevalent.

Marketers cannot have it both ways. They cannot bask in the glory of what in recent years they have enjoyed calling "relationship marketing," while ignoring—even trampling on—the needs and rights of some of our most vulnerable citizens.

1. Is there a moral dimension connected with credit card issuers sending out several *billion* solicitations every year? Explain.

2. Whose responsibility is it to protect the mentally disabled who are able to live on their own from the problems associated with credit card abuse? Families and friends? Government? Welfare organizations? Marketers? Give the reasons for your answer.

PRODUCTS

Introduction

If marketing is all about exchanges, then what is exchanged—the product (or the service or the idea)—must be at the heart of marketing. Long before the four P's of marketing, and before mass media advertising, sales promotion tactics, and distribution channels, there were products being exchanged, and often there were moral problems attendant on those exchanges.

Perhaps the most obvious of these problems is the question of product liability: Who bears the responsibility when a product harms the consumer or, more broadly, harms society (e.g., the environment)? To what extent should the buyer be held responsible when the product harms the buyer, or others, or society after the exchange has been made? The concept *caveat emptor*, "let the buyer beware," has a long history, and though it has been limited drastically both legally and ethically, it is far from dead. Caveat emptor still represents a rock-solid position at one end of the wide spectrum of ideas on this subject of product liability. The rationale behind the concept is individual responsibility: The buyer has the obligation to become well informed about the product before the sale because, when he or she enters into the sales agreement, liability for any harm done passes to the buyer.

At the other end of the spectrum lies the concept of absolute liability: After the seller has introduced a product into the stream of commerce, the seller should be held responsible when the product does *any* harm to individuals or to society. In the most extreme form of this concept, the seller retains that responsibility for as long as the product is in use. The rationale is that the seller has the best chance of preventing harm because the seller knows more about the product than anyone else does. Thus, the seller has the obligation to make any necessary alterations to the product to prevent harm to consumers. It is also argued that the seller has a greater incentive and a better opportunity to make those changes.

However, this issue has almost as many shades of gray as the marketplace has products. Some products, such as chain saws, are inherently dangerous every time they are used. Tobacco products cause millions of deaths each year around the world, but they represent a different type of danger to individuals and society. Even as benign a product as aspirin causes a few deaths. So we must make judgments as to how many of these deaths are "acceptable" and somehow weigh the benefits of pain relief to millions against the costs of death to a few.

There is also the question: If the seller knows how to make a product safer, is the seller obligated to do so? Whether the product is seat belts and air bags in automobiles or safety shields on chain saws, is the seller responsible for adding these features to the product, always incurring some additional cost, or must the seller simply make them available to the buyer as an option? In this case, the "free" market falls short of society's expectations. Both buyer and seller might be perfectly happy about the exchange of an automobile without seat belts, but for social (and perhaps macroeconomic) reasons, seat belts must be added to automobiles.

Questions such as the following also add shades of gray:

- ◆Did an aberration in the manufacturing process that produced the faulty product harm the consumer, or did the actual design of the faulty product cause the harm, which means that all such products are harmful?
- ◆What was the intent of the manufacturer/seller, and did the seller make a reasonable effort to avoid making a faulty product?
- ◆How much can a seller reasonably expect a buyer to know about the product and its use? This question takes on special significance in the global marketplace. Consider the problems associated for so long with the marketing of infant formula in developing countries. Can illiterate mothers of newborn babies in Africa know that purified water must be used with the formula? Can they be expected to know that in almost all cases, breast-feeding is far better for the baby, despite the advertising messages that formula is the modern, Western way?

Even in the midst of these intractable questions, we can be sure of one thing: The distinction between right and wrong, whether determined by the legal system or by public opinion, is constantly shifting. Furthermore, it is my contention that this distinction is constantly shifting toward increased responsibility of the seller. This makes things doubly difficult for sellers. They face not only uncertainty, but also increasing societal expectations.

Questions about liability are not the only product-related ethical issues that concern marketers. At least two issues involve product packaging. Do marketers have an obligation to reduce waste by holding packaging to a minimum? There is a growing belief among environmentalists that they do, and though reducing waste has not become a major issue yet in the United States, it certainly has in Germany, where strict regulations require the recycling of *all* packaging.

Another packaging issue is the occasional practice of "downsizing." Let's say that a cereal manufacturer, along with all its major competitors in the industry, has a 32-ounce size package in its line. The manufacturer decides that it can add to its profit margin if it puts only 29 ounces of cereal in the same-size box. To avoid breaking the law, it labels the new box as containing 29 ounces, but the typeface of this information is small, and many or most buyers will not read it. Buyers will assume that the box they have bought over and over again still contains the same amount of cereal. What are the ethical considerations of such a tactic?

Moving beyond products that are or can be harmful in the usual sense, what about products that significant groups in society deem inappropriate? Examples are video games that feature violent themes, rap music that urges killing cops and drug use, or even state lottery games. Some of these questions will be dealt with in the section "Inappropriate Marketing."

Finally, a new category of product issues has emerged in the last decade: the working conditions under which products are made. Nike, Wal-Mart, and Kathie Lee Gifford have all discovered that many consumers are concerned about this issue. No one claims that the product is harmful to the buyer. Instead, the contention is that society—the global society—is harmed in the manufacturing of the product. Regardless of what we think is a proper living wage for workers in Korean shoe factories, marketers have learned that this issue must be addressed.

There is at least one common thread running through all of these ethical issues: The buyer must be well-informed about the product. This was a relatively simple matter 150 years ago. Consider the market for transportation, which in the eighteenth century meant buying a horse. A prudent buyer could look at a horse and make an informed judgment as to its value: its age, its health, its strength, its speed, and so on. Today, transportation means buying an automobile, and the average buyer has no way on his or her own of making an informed judgment about the merits of one car versus another. The buyer must rely either on what the seller claims or on the advice of some trusted third party, such as a consumer advocacy group. The problem may be even more extreme in other product categories such as computers, wireless telephones, or prescription drugs. The wonders of technology have brought us an array of extraordinary products that have the potential of satisfying needs and wants in ways unimaginable a few decades ago. But that same technology has left the individual buyer at an unfair disadvantage in the marketplace. The seller knows everything; the buyer knows almost nothing. This creates a surefire breeding ground for ethical problems.

The following essays call attention to at least some of these issues in a variety of industry settings.

5

A Debate on the Need for Regulation

At a conference in Boston a few years ago, I had a chance to chat with a friend and colleague who had both good news and bad news for me. The good news was that she read my essays regularly. The bad news was that she disagreed with me just as regularly.

I have consistently argued that marketers must take greater responsibility for the harm their products may cause. To prevent or minimize that harm, they must take more care in the design of products, hold to the highest standards in manufacturing, and accept responsibility when harm does occur without resorting to bullying tactics and expensive legal maneuvering.

Two specific objections that my colleague mentioned are closely related. First, she believes that the focus of marketing ethics should be personal responsibility, and in her mind that means the consumer. Second, she believes that marketers must concentrate on "the demand side" to solve marketing problems. Because there will always be some firm to supply what consumers want, she recommends that consumers be educated and encouraged to demand what is good for them individually and what is good for society.

In principle, it is difficult to disagree with either of these views. I, too, am a firm believer in individual responsibility. We should not automatically blame the manufacturer when consumers' reckless or thoughtless use of products leads to accidents. Individual responsibility does indeed apply to consumers. I would, however, extend that application to managers and marketing decision makers as well. I also believe in the absolute necessity of consumer education and in the wisdom of giving consumers the greatest possible degree of free choice.

But, where is it written that the issues of product liability and consumer protection must be approached from only one direction? Marketing executives should be expected to exercise restraint and use good judgment, and the same should be expected of consumers. It is not too much

30

to caution marketers to adopt minimal standards for product safety, avoid price gouging, and communicate honestly with their customers.

My colleague is a top-notch scholar and teacher, and I am certain that she too is searching for the public good. We both want a system that is moral. Yet the market in itself is amoral; therefore, a moral system and the public good, however defined, cannot be achieved by relying entirely on the workings of the market. Marketing executives must either act sometimes in ways that are not totally driven by the maximization of profits or expect some level of social or government control.

There is ample historical evidence for these concerns. Various Mediterranean cultures of biblical times warned about the dishonest use of weights and measures. Frontier stories from the nineteenth-century American West tell of "snake oil" salesmen and others pitching phony schemes on hapless or careless buyers. The history of business affairs is replete with stories of the predatory practices of sellers.

If what we strive for is a level playing field—an exchange process into which buyers and sellers can come together with some sort of equal standing, as Adam Smith envisioned—then it is not too much to expect that in addition to providing information and education for buyers, sellers must exercise restraint. If they do not do so voluntarily, society, through various levels of government, will mandate it.

As soon as the subject of government controls is raised, I know that my colleague would remind me of the long list of government mistakes and excesses. Each of us has a list of what I call "horror stories"—examples of product liability regulation that seem to ignore even a modest level of good sense on the part of the buyer, or ineffectual government-mandated product-labeling requirements that sometimes do more harm than good. Government regulations can indeed be silly; they are always costly and sometimes even dangerous. But they can also be effective, and sometimes they are absolutely necessary to protect the public health.

The answer is not to reject government regulations in principle, but to improve both the process and the output of public policymaking so that mistakes are avoided. We need, and can achieve, a better batting average: fewer strikeouts and more home runs in our consumer-protection public policy. We will need it even more in the future. Two important reasons are made patently clear by the interactions and relationships between manufacturers and retailers on the one hand and consumers on the other hand. First, sellers continue to grow in both size and power relative to buyers. Second, the products they exchange are becoming more complex and technical in nature. Both of these trends bode ill for those who honestly want to achieve that level playing field.

We must search for ways to educate consumers and provide them with better information so that they can become more intelligent purchasers and users. We must also expect consumers to use good judgment. However, I hold out the further expectation that sellers, too, should exercise good judgment and that they should make decisions based not solely on the consequences to their profits but also on the consequences to society. I call for firms to break out of the box of one-dimensional, bottom-line thinking and the limitations of the amoral market and incorporate a moral dimension to their marketing planning and implementation.

It is too simplistic to recite the mantra, "Get government off the back of business." Government regulation is necessary when consumers are unlikely or unable to help themselves. This is hardly a radical manifesto for the technologically complex, size- and power-based times in which we live and market our products.

1. Give examples that either support or refute the argument that consumers need help from the government because (a) sellers are becoming more powerful and (b) products are becoming more complex and difficult to understand.

2. With more emphasis on education, will consumers demand safer products?

Dangerous Products: Tobacco

From 1997 to 1998, there was a great stirring of political, legal, public health, advocacy, and corporate groups that were attempting to reach some sort of agreement on tobacco issues, including the marketing of cigarettes. After four decades of growing public awareness of the health dangers of tobacco (smoking causes more than 400,000 deaths per year in the United States alone) and years of regulations hampered by the foot-dragging and intransigence of the cigarette companies, these groups tried to hammer out what they called a "comprehensive settlement."

Anti-tobacco advocates, public health officials, and even some politicians wanted to implement a sensible regulatory framework for this product—to control or eliminate the harmful substances in tobacco and place tighter controls on cigarette marketing—and to recover at least some of the public health costs from the companies whose products were responsible. The chances of crippling law suits, which were once believed impossible, had grown to the point that cigarette manufacturers were willing to negotiate a settlement that would put some acceptable limits on their liability for past injuries and allow them to continue making and selling cigarettes, albeit under stricter regulations.

All of this came to naught. The comprehensive settlement talks collapsed amidst a flurry of finger-pointing and laying blame. However, it is useful to explore some issues about dangerous products in general against this background. For example, it is unresolved how much responsibility manufacturers and sellers must bear for the harms caused by the products they introduce into the stream of commerce. It is also unresolved as to when and to what extent the government must intervene in the marketplace to protect consumers from unsafe products. Who then should decide whether products are unsafe—sellers, buyers, advocates, or the government?

Issue # 1

What can be done about products that are inherently dangerous? Anti-tobacco activists argue that cigarettes and other tobacco products are fundamentally different from any other product because they are dangerous *even when used as intended*. There is no safe method or level of usage. Even so, there are plenty of other products on the market today that present some level of danger for some customers: alcoholic beverages, gambling, violence and sex in entertainment, fatty foods, and motorcycles, to name a few products most often cited.

The United States' unhappy and unsuccessful experience with Prohibition in the 1920s has led policymakers to reject almost categorically even the discussion of a total ban on the sale of cigarettes. We still believe in individual responsibility, the right to make mistakes, and the right to act in foolhardy ways that may be harmful. At some point, however, those individual rights conflict with the rights of others. In the case of cigarettes, that point is reached with second-hand smoke and the harm it does to nonsmokers. Another point of conflict is the enormous public health costs of smoking-related illnesses that smokers impose on society. The proposed compromise would have allowed tobacco companies to continue marketing cigarettes under much tighter regulations and adults to continue buying them. At the same time, it would have required the manufacturers to finance public awareness campaigns, which would hold the number of smokers to a minimum, and pay billions of dollars toward the public health costs already incurred.

Issue # 2

Should so-called vulnerable groups be protected, and if so, how? In recent years, much of the emphasis of the anti-tobacco groups has been directed at protecting children. There are two reasons for this: One is strategic, the other political. Strategically, it makes sense to target public policy efforts—education about the health consequences, enforcement of minimum-age restrictions on purchasing cigarettes—at teens and preteens. This is because the vast majority of smokers, 80%–90%, begin smoking before they are 18 years of age. As many as 40% take up the habit and become addicted by the time they are 14 years of age.

Politically, in the broadest sense, advocates have discovered that adult smokers do not generate much sympathy; in contrast, there is great public outrage over the prospect of children becoming addicted to tobacco. Where there is outrage, there is greater potential for significant funding from foundations and concerned individuals. Tobacco companies consistently run into a buzz saw of adverse public opinion when they target groups that society perceives as vulnerable: children, minorities, women, and less-educated groups in developing countries.

Issue # 3

Should the marketing and advertising of this dangerous product be regulated? There is not much debate about this question any more. Now the debate is about how and how much to regulate. Long ago in the United States, tobacco advertising was banned from television and radio, and the government mandated health warnings on cigarette packages. More recently, cigarette ads were banned on billboards and in sports arenas. (Throughout much of Europe, *all* tobacco advertising is prohibited.) There is considerable disagreement whether such advertising encourages nonsmokers to begin smoking and whether advertising restrictions have any public health impact, but there is widespread acceptance of such restrictions, if only for symbolic reasons. The prevailing sentiment is that even if society cannot ban the product, at least the marketing of it should be banned or restricted. Predictably, the tobacco industry and its supporters take the opposite view: If the product can be sold legally, the manufacturers have the right to promote it.

Issue # 4

How should corporations be punished? In announcing the settlement, Michael Moore, the Attorney General of Mississippi, declared that the tobacco companies ought to be punished for their past conduct. Society has paid too little attention to this question. Let's raise some of the more important issues.

Because society cannot send a corporation to jail, should guilt be assigned to individual executives, and should society penalize them? This is not impossible, but it is extremely difficult given the complex decision-making processes in organizations. Punishing corporations, therefore, must take the form of monetary fines. But who in the long run pays those fines? The government pays them, at least in part, because the fines are a tax-deductible expense. But the intent of the penalty is not to give corporations a tax break. The shareholders? That would hardly be a just or effective consequence. If the corporation is punished to such an extent that its very existence is threatened, then its employees, its suppliers, and the communities in which it does business are all are hurt by the penalty; this is not the intent of society either. How society assigns guilt and then penalizes the guilty to deter corporate managers from committing future criminal activity is no simple matter.

A comprehensive settlement of tobacco issues that includes marketing problems—for example, Food and Drug Administration authority, more effective warning labels, campaigns to reduce teenage smoking—was a possibility in 1998, but it was never realized, and so the industry, its critics, and the government will be wrestling with these problems for the foreseeable future. What progress is made toward a resolution will depend on how the involved parties come to grips with the fundamental issues surrounding responsibility for product liability. Adult consumers must accept responsibility for legal products they use inappropriately or abuse. Advocacy groups and the government can be expected to offer warnings and protection. But, at some point and to some degree, manufacturers and sellers must also share in the responsibility for the harm done by their products. Caveat emptor as a governing principle between buyers and sellers is dead. Marketers must adapt to a new moral doctrine.

1. If cigarettes are as much of a danger to the public health as the statistics suggest, should they be made illegal?

2. Are there effective and fair ways to penalize corporations? Explain.

7

Brand Identities: Do Consumers Need to Know?

In 1998, a new long-distance service was launched. Simply dial 10-10-345 and place your calls through Lucky Dog Telephone Co., the newspaper and subway card ads told the public. Fed up with dealing with giant companies such as AT&T, MCI, and Sprint? Just switch to Lucky Dog, and you'll love the small company–style friendly and efficient service.

Well, not quite. It turned out that Lucky Dog was in fact a subsidiary of AT&T, which was something the telecommunications behemoth was not eager to share with the public. AT&T wanted to attract a younger, hipper customer, one who would not be attracted to venerable old Ma Bell. This raises interesting questions about what consumers have a right to know, what they need to know, and what they want to know.

Forty years ago, President John F. Kennedy proposed his so-called Consumers' Bill of Rights. Prominent among those rights was the consumer's right to information about the product or service, along with the right to safe products, the right of choice, and the right to be heard. Virtually no one would argue with the consumer's right to be informed, but as the saying goes, the devil is in the details. Just how much information does the consumer need in order to satisfy a corporation's social responsibility and marketing ethics concerns?

There are no blanket rules, and there are no easy answers to that question. But that does not mean the question can be ignored. It means that marketing decision makers need to work a little harder to answer it at any given time, and the answer will differ from one corporation to the next. How much information needs to be provided depends on what the product or service in question is, who the consumer is, and whether that consumer is knowledgeable and of mature judgment. It will depend on how much harm might result if the consumer does not have the information, as well as the nature and likelihood of that harm. In other words, there is a vast difference between the need to provide information that might save a life or prevent a serious accident and the need to provide information that would merely save the consumer a minor inconvenience.

Back to Lucky Dog and the long distance telephone industry. Lucky Dog and other "dial around" telephone carriers became an increasingly important factor in that industry. They enabled customers to dial around the big firms—AT&T, MCI, and Sprint—and place their calls through supposedly small companies that offered better deals than the giants. But the giants grew tired of losing business to the smaller firms, especially because the newcomers' prices, which were too confusing for most consumers to compare, were no lower. So, to compete, MCI created 10-10-321. Initially, AT&T derided MCI for keeping its corporate parentage a secret. However, AT&T continued to lose long-distance business. So, following the "if you can't beat 'em, join 'em" strategy, AT&T decided to launch its own flanker brand, Lucky Dog.

There are plenty of pure marketing questions to generate a good case discussion. Was it a good idea for AT&T, one of the most widely recognized brand names in the country, to spend its resources establishing and promoting a competing brand? Would Lucky Dog cannibalize AT&T's business to such an extent that no gain in net market share would be worth the expense of the launch? In this essay, however, let's stick with the ethics and social responsibility questions.

Most consumers, I believe, are unaware of the relationship between brands and corporate parents when the parent chooses to pursue an individual branding policy. How many consumers know, for example, that Jif, Aleve, Tide, Pampers, Crest, and Folgers all come from Procter & Gamble, even though the P&G name is on every package in small print? How many people know or care that Doritos and all those other snacks from Frito-Lay are part of the PepsiCo family? Do customers at Banana Republic or Old Navy stores care or need to know that both groups are divisions of Gap Inc.?

In the beer industry, there is a similar situation to the AT&T/Lucky Dog case. Miller, which is a division of Philip Morris, created the Plank Road label to compete in the rapidly growing microbrew segment of the market. It was clear that an increasing number of beer drinkers wanted something different from what the leading brands were offering, whether for reasons of taste, snob appeal, or some other factor. The segment of the market that was moving toward Fat Tire, Sam Adams, Pete's Wicked Ale, and a host of other microbrewery labels would never be satisfied with a new beer under the Miller family brand name. Thus, with no mention of its parentage, Plank Road was born. Anheuser-Busch followed the same strategy with its Red Wolf brand.

Is it unethical for Miller to market Plank Road beer in a way that the buyer believes that it comes from a small brewer? Is it important for the buyer to know that Plank Road is really a product of Miller or for the long-distance dialer of 10-10-345 to know that Lucky Dog is really AT&T under a different guise? Do those customers have a *right* to that knowledge?

In those situations, the answer is no, because there are no significant adverse consequences. No harm is likely to ensue; no significant rights are denied.

There are other situations, however, that raise more difficult questions. Is it important for consumers who add Kraft, General Foods, and Nabisco products to their shopping baskets to know that those brands are all part of Philip Morris, the world's largest manufacturer and seller of cigarettes? It is clear enough why Philip Morris does not want its benign grocery products to be tainted with the stigma of tobacco. But there are many anti-tobacco advocates who might switch to other brands if they knew that their purchases of Kraft cheese and Oreo and Chips Ahoy cookies fattened the coffers of the marketer of the Marlboro Man.

There has also been some controversy around Miramax, the producer of many R-rated movies. It is not widely known that Miramax is a division of Disney, and Disney makes no effort to publicize the relationship to the movie-going public. Again, the reason is clear enough. There might be considerable damage to Disney's squeaky-clean, family-oriented image if its role in the production and promotion of adult-themed movies with high quotients of violence and sex were known.

However, even when we consider the examples of Philip Morris and Disney, the marketing strategies of downplaying or even hiding the connection between the brand and its true parent are problematic but not unethical. They are maddening to critics of cigarettes and of violence in films, but there is little harm done by keeping the corporate relationships under wraps. Of course, the critics can and do find their own ways of publicizing the relationships as widely as possible, sometimes even calling for boycotts of all the firm's brands and product lines. The strategies may be mildly deceptive in not revealing the "whole truth," and consumers do have a right to be informed, but they have other sources of getting that information.

It is impossible to tell customers *everything* about products and how they are made. Just how much information must be provided is one of the most pervasive ethical questions facing marketers, and it ranges from the ingredients and side effects of prescription drugs to the age of workers in soccer ball factories in Pakistan. In each example, the answer to this ethical question depends on how harmful the product may be to the consumer and how important it is for the consumer to know.

1. Was it deceptive for AT&T to hide its parentage of Lucky Dog, and if so, is this deception ethically wrong?

2. How much responsibility should Philip Morris take to inform consumers that the maker of Oreo cookies also produces Marlboro cigarettes? How much responsibility should consumers take?

A New Dimension of Morality in Marketing

8

O ver the past decade, a growing problem has created an entirely new dimension of marketing ethics. It is no longer sufficient that products in and of themselves are well-designed, safe, and properly made for their intended use: Firms must now ensure that those products are made under fair working conditions. Globalization and outsourcing have become more the rule than the exception in business. Thus, sellers must now account for the working conditions and the wages paid in the factories where their products are made—whether those factories are owned and operated by the seller or by outside contractors and suppliers.

Levi Strauss, which takes great pride in its reputation for a consistently high level of business ethics, now insists that its contractors, whether in Latin America or Southeast Asia, follow strict contractual terms that go well beyond the number of stitches to the inch in each garment. Levi's contracts now spell out standards for the minimum age of employees, overtime pay, plant safety, and healthy and humane working conditions.

This is not strictly an international issue. Apparel manufacturers in New York, San Francisco, and Los Angeles have long turned a blind eye to the squalid, cramped working conditions of their Chinatown contractors·and subcontractors. And several years ago it was discovered that the immigrant laborers who pick strawberries in the fields near Watsonville, Calif., were living in cardboard carton shacks on the periphery of those fields and sometimes in bare caves dug into the ground, with no sanitation facilities whatsoever. The growers who hired the pickers were owners of small businesses and did not have the capital to provide decent housing. There were also growers who paid substandard wages and ignored other employment laws and regulations. The large corporations that bought the berries from the growers—the local "coolers," food processors such as Smucker's, and retailers such as Safeway—all denied any responsibility because the pickers were not their employees.

It is difficult enough for marketers and managers to reach a consensus regarding the extent of their responsibilities to their own employees. If they make sure that their own employees receive a decent wage and work under reasonable conditions, is that enough? Hanging in the air is the Old Testament query, "Am I my brother's keeper?" The idea that marketers must now accept responsibility for what their suppliers and contractors do—the wages they pay, the people they hire, the working conditions of their factories and shops—adds an extraordinary new dimension to the concept of corporate social responsibility.

International trade will surely continue to grow as the European Union becomes stronger and more consolidated, the North American Free Trade Agreement (NAFTA) expands its influence, and a new round of multilateral talks lowers trade barriers around the world even further. And so this new dimension of ethics and responsibility—a concern for the benefits and working conditions of a firm's suppliers and contractors—will also become more important. It is, however, fraught with difficult, unanswered questions that fall into four categories.

1. What constitutes unacceptable employment practices and working conditions? Considerable attention has focused on "slave labor" and "prison labor" conditions in China. Few people outside the Chinese government disagree that these are abhorrent practices and that we should not import and profit from merchandise made under such conditions, but the political problems of dealing with such matters have proved rather sticky. International agreement on new labor standards would be even more difficult to achieve. Although almost every nation in the world outlaws the use of child labor, in many countries there is little or no enforcement. There is also little agreement on some of the specifics—minimum age, physical demands of the job, or education alternatives. Even the United States exempts family farms from child labor laws. Harder still would be to reach international agreement on a minimum or living wage for a given economy or what benefits are essential in that economy.

2. Just when does a product become tainted or unacceptable? For example, if a woman's dress has been cut and sewn by 12- and 13-year-old girls in Honduras, retailers might all agree that ethical standards prohibit them from marketing the dress. But what if the body of the dress is produced under appropriate conditions in the manufacturer's own factory in the United States and just the shoulder pads (or the belt or the buttons) are imported from suppliers whose working conditions are not acceptable? What then are a retailer's ethical obligations?

3. How far back along the supply chain do a marketer's responsibilities extend? Just to the suppliers and contractors? To the suppliers of the suppliers and to the subcontractors of the contractors?

4. What is an importer's responsibility for policing the conditions in its contractors' factories? Levi Strauss does not simply include the specifications for such conditions in its contracts. It also hires its own regional supervisors to monitor plant safety and working conditions along with the quality of the actual garments.

These are troublesome questions; acceptable answers and a degree of consensus will not come easily. But the warning flags have been raised. Wal-Mart has been embarrassed more than once by selling merchandise manufactured by children earning $.05 an hour in Bangladesh, where there are no child labor laws, and by selling apparel made in Latin American factories with deplorable working conditions.

Nike and Nordstrom, along with Levi Strauss, have taken the lead in developing policies for managing this issue, though their policies are not necessarily appropriate for other importers. Nevertheless, all manufacturers and retailers involved in international purchasing are now confronted with this new moral dimension. They must not ignore it because it will not go away.

1. The new dimension of morality extends a business's responsibility beyond its own employees. What are the economic and ethical problems if a business ignores it?

2. Does Levi Strauss have the right to intervene in how an independent contractor conducts its own business? What if that independent contractor complies not only with the laws of its own country but also with its customs and culture?

9

Marketers Must Accept Greater Responsibilities

On a trip to Germany not long ago, my wife and I visited the old city of Freiburg, where the main attractions are the thirteenth-century cathedral and the outdoor market in the surrounding square. At the market our attention was captured by row after row, display after display of fresh vegetables, flowers, and fruits. Here were big, beautiful cauliflowers, leeks, potatoes, cabbages, squashes, and countless other varieties of produce spread on rough plank tables and watched over by the proud growers.

Perhaps it was the old European setting, but watching the customers choose their vegetables, with an occasional question for the vendor, made me think of what the buyer–seller relationship must have been like in Adam Smith's eighteenth-century Scotland. I had the sensation of being transported back to a time when buyer and seller came together with equal knowledge of the product. Shoppers examined the goods and would move on to another vendor's display if the produce there looked riper or juicier. Sellers' prices were quickly adjusted; they tended to be the same unless one grower's produce was obviously bigger or fresher.

There was no need for warning labels, complex warranties, instruction manuals, return policies, or 24-hour toll-free customer service lines. What you saw was what you got, and the buyers knew how to judge the value of the produce. How comforting for the buyer not to worry about whether the product was all it seemed to be or as it had been advertised or whether it might be dangerous, defective, or not worth the price.

Today, in a considerably more complex marketplace, there are at least three good reasons for marketers to accept greater responsibility for the interests of consumers: It can forestall government regulation, it can provide business with greater long-term profits by establishing a competitive advantage, and it is the right thing to do. In this more complex world, consumers rarely find selling conditions like those in the Freiburg marketplace.

Now, moving up and down the aisles of supermarkets, consumers must worry about what really is in the cans, boxes, and bottles that line the shelves. Even if they read the mandatory labels, will they understand what the ingredients are? How much sodium is healthy? Are food coloring and other additives harmful? Just what is autolyzed yeast anyway? Are cellulose powder, potassium sorbate, and calcium disodium natural products, and even if they are, are they nutritious? Did the milk come from cows that were fed bovine growth hormones, and if so, are those hormones dangerous? Has the meat been irradiated? Do customers want it if it has been? Do they want if it has not?

When twenty-first–century consumers shop for apparel, other questions come to mind. What does "made in the U.S.A." really mean? Was the garment assembled or the individual pieces cut or knit in the United States? Was the cloth woven from cotton grown in Alabama? Under what working conditions was the garment made, and were the seamstresses paid a decent wage? If consumers want the answers to those questions, who could provide them? The salesperson? The buyer? The store manager?

How many consumers have even the most rudimentary knowledge of high-tech products such as computers, automobiles, or even kitchen appliances? What is the true value of traction control or anti-lock braking systems in new cars? Do all the well-known computer brands have basically the same internal workings, as a CompUSA salesperson confessed, so it does not really matter what brand a consumer chooses?

The same or similar problems present themselves in the purchasing of services. What layperson can judge the difference in value between a will or a contract that is drawn up by a high-priced lawyer and a similar document from a lawyer who charges only half as much? Can a consumer make an informed judgment about whether a physician's advice is worth the fee?

These concerns are not new, but they are far removed in time and distance from the Freiburg outdoor market and certainly from Adam Smith's typical buyer–seller exchange. Of course, consumers do not want to return to the simpler days of the thirteenth, eighteenth, or even twentieth century. They are unwilling to give up modern technology and products that do wondrous things, even if they are unable to understand and judge the safety and value of those products.

Thus, we have a situation in which the exchange relationship is out of balance because the buyer has less information than the seller. Some would argue that if the free enterprise system is working, competition prevents sellers from harming or taking advantage of buyers. This works some of the time. However, there are other situations in which society does not want to wait for the slow-moving market to correct itself and weed out the unethical seller or in which too much harm can occur from even one problem, such as faulty automobile tires. In these cases, the government is typically called on to protect the consumer with new agencies, commissions, laws, and regulations. Consumer protection has a long history, but the results have not been perfect, and there are always warnings that the costs of such regulations to the business community are too great to bear.

Like it or not, business is faced with the reality that the need for consumer protection will continue to grow as products and services become increasingly complex. Sellers may decide that it is in their best interest to provide buyers with safe products and understandable information about their offerings, because it will obviate additional costly bureaucratic regulations, because they can create a competitive advantage by doing so, or perhaps even because it is the right thing to do.

1. Of the products you and your family purchase, which ones do you believe you know at least roughly as well as the seller?

2. Even if you do not really understand how a computer or an automobile works, how much information does the seller have a responsibility to provide to you?

Consumers Have Responsibilities, Too

Invariably, in discussions about marketing ethics, it is the sellers' actions that come under consideration. But buyers, as well as sellers, have moral responsibilities, and it is important to focus the spotlight now and then on whether buyers use whatever power or advantage they have in fair and responsible ways.

There are at least two types of problems to explore. The first occurs when a buyer takes advantage of a seller's return or exchange policy. Anyone who has experience in the retail apparel business is aware of the customer who buys—or, so to speak, borrows—a dress on Friday and returns it for full credit on Monday, even though it was obviously worn over the weekend. There are any number of stories about customers of Nordstrom, L.L.Bean, and other stores with well-publicized liberal return policies who return merchandise years after it was purchased or about customers who ask for and often receive credit for merchandise purchased from an entirely different store.

Although these firms may benefit in the long run from the good public relations these return policies generate, there is little question regarding the ethics of the customers' behavior. In most of those cases, the buyer has basically lied to the store by claiming that the merchandise did not fit or did not perform satisfactorily when, in fact, it did.

There is another category of buyer behavior that is more complex, interesting, and important to consider: if the buyer decides *not* to make a purchase on the basis of ethical or social considerations. This is an exercise of power of a different kind. For an individual buyer, this power is usually too weak to make an impact, but if many buyers agree to boycott—to cooperate in not buying a certain product or from a certain seller—the power is magnified. Withholding purchasing power in such a way aims to pressure the sellers into changing their patterns of doing business in some way.

On any given day, there are dozens of boycotts being waged against all kinds of firms for all sorts of reasons. Customers may be protesting companies for inhumane treatment of animals in the testing and development of their products, for perceived civil rights violations against women or minorities, for exploitation of natural resources, for layoffs, for exporting jobs, for selling unsafe products, for selling fur coats, and so on.

Most of these boycotts never attract much attention. Only a few gain any measurable support among consumers and are able to bring significant pressure on the organization to change its behavior. More than 30 years ago, Cesar Chavez organized an effective boycott against lettuce and grape growers in California to improve working conditions and wages for migrant farm workers. A 1970s boycott of Nestlé food products in the United States, triggered by Nestlé's aggressive marketing of infant formula in developing nations, also became a cause célèbre. Organized labor in the United States sometimes mounts campaigns to "Buy American" and punish firms that outsource production to other countries. These efforts have had little, if any, lasting effect.

Occasionally, an issue attracts considerable media attention, such as the story that Kathie Lee Gifford apparel, which is sold at Wal-Mart, was being made by Central American companies that pay their workers substandard wages and force them to work under inhumane working conditions. But the effect on consumer buying practices was short lived.

Why don't more of these ethically motivated protests and boycotts gain more attention and have a longer lasting impact? Is it because of a lack of information? Perhaps too few consumers know too little about these issues. They may never have known, or they may fail to remember, which of the thousands of products on the shelves of supermarkets and department stores have some sort of moral stigma attached to them. Which products are made with child or slave labor? Which products are made by companies that use cruel methods of animal testing? Which companies use contractors or subcontractors in Latin America or Asia that physically abuse their employees and punish those whose productivity falls below what is expected?

Is it for lack of caring? Consumers may simply dismiss these issues as inconsequential. Or perhaps the price of morality is too high. Buyers may be unwilling to pay an extra dollar or two for a shirt made in a factory that pays seamstresses a living wage. They may balk at paying $20 more for a rug made in factories that do not use child labor.

Some argue that such matters of conscience, morality, and ethical behavior really have no place in the exchange transactions between buyers and sellers. Typically, all that matters to buyers is the products' quality and price. If these factors meet buyers' requirements, they make the purchase. But shouldn't the seller's (or the manufacturer's) ethical behavior be considered an important attribute of the product as well? Buyers who ignore such factors are complicit and complaisant. Buyers should exercise ethical judgment and economic judgment. To ignore such matters is nothing less than moral laziness.

It is commonplace in the world of marketing to expect sellers to abide by certain ethical standards. But buyers too have moral obligations and responsibilities, especially to be informed about the seller's ethical behavior and to consider it carefully and thoughtfully when deciding whether to make a purchase.

1. How much more, if any, would you be willing to pay for a pair of athletic shoes if you could be assured that those shoes were produced in factories where working conditions were humane and workers were paid a living wage?

2. What problems make it difficult for buyers to be well informed about the moral behavior of manufacturers and the stores that sell their products?

PRICING

Introduction

In the exchange transaction of a product or service, nothing is so fundamental as the concept of price. The very idea of an exchange assumes a price that is paid, whether in goods or currency. Long before sellers worried about how to promote a product—how and where to advertise it, whether to offer coupons or free samples—they needed a price. Before sellers worried about how to distribute the product—whether to sell through a broker, wholesalers, or retailers or sell directly to customers—they needed a price. No doubt, business historians can identify when promotion and distribution became two of the four P's of marketing, but price has been there from the very beginning.

Because this book is a search for the moral dimension of marketing, and because price is such an integral part of marketing, there must be a moral dimension of pricing as well. The phrase "fair price" is often used, and it carries a moral connotation, so perhaps it would be a good place to start. What is a fair price, or what makes a price fair?

When I ask my students this question, some revert to what they dimly remember from their economics textbooks. They suggest that it is where the supply and demand curves cross, where supply equals demand. Because both buyer and seller agree to this price, in theory, does that make it fair? I often counter this question with examples from the pharmaceutical industry or with examples of desperately needed products such as water after a natural disaster, in which the temporary spike in demand might be expected to drive the price up well beyond what society would consider fair. In its quest to become more quantitative and more like the "hard" sciences, perhaps economics has detached itself from the social sciences and shed any pretensions of morality.

If the definition of a fair price is elusive, perhaps it is the perception of fairness that is important. Consider the process of buying a new or used automobile. Traditionally, this process has involved bargaining between buyer and seller. The seller wants the most profitable transaction, but the seller also wants the buyer to believe that the price is fair and that he or she has received a good deal. The more complex the deal—for example, if it involves a trade-in or financing, with its complicated calculus of interest rates, length of the loan, balloon payments, and leasing provisions—the easier the seller can create an illusion of fairness and the more difficult it is for the buyer to know whether he or she has been treated fairly.

Most customers know what the opposite of fairness is, and it is called gouging. Most customers, however, have little knowledge with which to judge whether a retailer has set an unreasonably or abnormally high price on a product. Many buyers are outraged to learn, for example, that a department store routinely charges $100 or more for a sweater for which it paid only $50: In other words, they consider it a 100% markup, even though it is only a 50% markup to a retailer, based on the retail price. Customers do not calculate the substantial payroll, real estate, advertising, and other costs the store must bear to be able to offer that sweater in attractive surroundings with even a modest level of customer service.

Even if we were to accept that the $100 price for the sweater is reasonable, that it is not gouging, let's carry the example one step further. What if the manufacturer wants to unload its entire inventory of these sweaters and sells them to the retailer at half the usual price, which means that the retailer pays only $25 for each sweater? Now the retailer must decide what price to put on these sweaters. Perhaps the store will advertise a special sale and offer the sweaters for only $50. The customer is pleased to buy the sweater at half its regular price, the retailer is pleased because it is still getting its normal markup, and the manufacturer is pleased to reduce its excess inventory.

If the sweater has been selling well at $100, however, the retailer may decide to continue selling the sweaters at that price. Now the store is receiving a 75% markup in retail terms (or a 300% markup in the customers' minds). Presumably, the customer is pleased to buy the sweater at this price. The retailer is very pleased, though the retailer would argue that the extra profit on this sweater only makes up for the losses on other purchases that were not so popular. But is this gouging? The customer would probably say yes because the store makes a higher than normal profit margin on this sweater. The retailer would say no because of the losses on other items.

The retailer, of course, is not always in control. Customers know that merchandise will eventually be marked down—for example, just before Christmas—so they may choose to wait for the sale price before buying. They may sacrifice selection for price. In recent decades, this has become an increasingly familiar pattern, and department and specialty stores still struggle to adapt their merchandising tactics to accommodate this trend.

These examples depict both the buyer and the seller jockeying for advantage; therefore, they seem to support the idea that marketing is fundamentally an adversarial relationship. The seller will be satisfied if at the end of the season or the year, profit and return on investment are satisfactory. The buyer's satisfaction will depend more on emotion and perceptions. Regardless of the buyer's satisfaction on the day of purchase, if the store marks the sweater down the next day, the buyer will feel manipulated. In buying a new car, the buyer's satisfaction will depend not only on the price and deal that was negotiated but also on the feeling that the deal was as good or better than anyone else's. The search for a fair price is no simple task; we do not know how to incorporate subjective feelings about satisfaction with the objective reality of supply and demand curves.

What we do know is that, at the very least, customers must understand the price to consider it fair. There must be no hidden gimmicks and no surprises. There must be transparency. As more and more disposable income goes to purchasing services rather than goods, these factors become even more important. Here are three examples.

First, how many consumers really understand the cost of the credit cards they use with such frequency and sometimes with such abandon? True enough, federal regulations now require that credit card issuers state the finance charges annually so that there is some uniformity among the different cards on this aspect of the price. But customers rarely read the fine print of the contracts they sign to get the cards, and it is there in those legalistic, mind-numbing details that the issuer is given the option of raising the annual finance charge percentage if the customer makes a late payment or for any one of many other reasons. Periodically, the issuers send out blank checks that encourage their customers to use them for "extra cash," but among all the blandishments and promotional material, it is almost impossible to find out how much it will cost to use those checks.

Second, consider the difficulty of understanding the cost of wireless telephone service. There are so many different factors that go into the final bill—roaming charges from within or outside the region, regular service charges, calls made at different times of the day or the week—that it is difficult at best to choose from among the competing services and to know whether to be satisfied with the price.

Third, think about the cost of health insurance. As vital as this service is, it is almost impossible for buyers to comprehend the intricacies of the price and whether they are getting what they want for a fair price. They must know how much their employer, or perhaps the government, is contributing and how much they are paying from their own pocket; they must be able to understand deductibles, co-pays, hospital versus outpatient charges, specialists both in- and outside a network, different charges for generic versus branded drugs, and so on.

To make intelligent purchasing decisions, buyers must clearly understand the true price of what the seller is offering. This understanding is not sufficient by itself, but it is necessary in arriving at a fair price. Thus, sellers have an obligation to price their goods and services in ways that will lead to clearer understanding. They should not obfuscate the price by attaching conditions in the fine print of a sales agreement. They should not confuse the customer by combining so many caveats and options that the actual price of the good or service is lost and can no longer be compared with competitive products. This is a small but important step in the process of turning marketing from an adversarial to a cooperative relationship.

Fair Price

The phrase "fair price" is used often enough that the meaning should be clear to me, but I am troubled whenever I try to really define it. Presumably, for a price to be considered fair, both buyer and seller would need to agree that it is. And therein lies the rub: If both the buyer and the seller are looking out for their own interest, how often or how easily can they arrive at a price that they both consider fair? What is the mechanism?

Economists, of course, have no problem here. They assume buyers and sellers enter into transactions of their own free will and, therefore, must be satisfied with the agreed-on price. Beyond that, fairness is not an issue with most economists; the market determines the price, and that is the end of the discussion. Marketers have a more difficult problem because they are interested in more than a single transaction. They want to keep customers for life—even trying to calculate the "lifetime value" of a customer—because keeping a customer is far less expensive than adding a new one. This requires a good bit more than just making a sale; it involves making sure the customer is satisfied, which includes the customer's perception that the price is fair.

A Scottish researcher, Sofia Daskou, has written an article in which she describes, among other things, various theories about exchanges (see Daskou 2000). One is that the buyer (and the seller, too, in different ways) should believe that he or she has received the "best deal" for the price and that all things considered—the product itself; the service before, during, and after the sale; timeliness; convenience of buying; and so forth—must add up to the best deal available or the customer will seek another seller next time. I do not want to oversimplify the matter—there are vast streams of literature on transaction costs and switching costs that marketers must consider when setting prices—but let's stick with the fundamentals.

Daskou describes another exchange theory that argues that both the buyer and the seller should believe that they have gotten about as good a deal as the other and that the agreed-on price was not significantly more beneficial to one than to the other. There needs to be a sense of equity in the transaction.

To my surprise, on the very same day I read Daskou's article, I was exposed to two situations that deal with customers' perceptions of fair prices. Situation number one: I drove into a local service station to fill up my car with gasoline. To my delight the price on the regular unleaded pump read $1.359, but unfortunately the pump was not operating. I drove to another pump where the price for the same gas was $1.489. This second price was not out of line with other signs I had seen along the way, but I still was not happy about paying the higher price. When I called this discrepancy to the attention of the cashier, he happily explained, "We just changed the prices a half hour ago, when the station across the road raised theirs."

Grudgingly, I paid the higher price. If I had arrived at the station only a half hour earlier, I would have saved almost $2.00! Or, if the first pump had been working, I might have saved the same amount. Wasn't it misleading to have the old price posted on the first pump? Did I really want to buy gas from this station in the future, even if it charged the same as the competing station across the road?

Situation number two: I read that Amazon.com had instituted a new promotion in which a customer could receive free shipping for ordering two or more items. At the same time, however, Amazon changed many of its prices, lowering them on some items but raising them on others. It was not long before customers became aware of these price changes and cried foul, complaining that Amazon was paying for the free shipping by charging more for the books and CDs. A company spokesperson described the price increases as a *reduction in the discount*. What a wonderful example of marketing double-talk.

These are two examples of pricing tactics that left at least some customers dissatisfied. Were the prices fair? Were the tactics unethical? Certainly a seller has the right to increase the price it charges for its product.

In the first example, although I was unhappy about paying the higher price for gasoline, I could not honestly claim that the service station had been unfair or unethical. The problem was mine, of course, because I had arrived a half hour too late. This is a problem that every retailer faces: how to satisfy customers who want to buy an item after a special price promotion but who resent paying the higher price. A retailer that is really concerned about maintaining good customer relationships will often make an exception if the customer complains and allow him or her to buy the item at the former lower price. The essential point is that I—and most customers of service stations, I presume—know that gasoline prices go up and down rather frequently, often in response to competitive pressures. I may have grumbled to myself about my bad luck, and I may have even blamed (perhaps unreasonably) the station, but in my heart of hearts I know that there are plenty of other examples in which I had the good luck to benefit from sale prices. My dissatisfaction was based on my belief that at that specific time, the station had profited *more* from the transaction than I had.

The second example is quite different. Although some customers were upset with Amazon's tactics, many others were not, especially if they were not aware of the price changes. For them, they had received about as good a deal from Amazon as from anyone else, considering that Amazon provides a customized service and a good Internet shopping experience and that most of us do not believe that Amazon profits more from the sale of a book than we do. However, to whatever extent Amazon's reduced discounts—or higher prices, in normal language— were designed to compensate for the free shipping policy, the company was guilty of false advertising. It was the marketing equivalent of the magician's sleight of hand: the left hand captures your attention while the right hand uncovers the hidden coin or colored scarf. Amazon captured its customers' attention with the promise of free shipping while raising some of its prices when customers were not looking in that direction. Under these circumstances, the new price was not fair, even with free shipping, and the transaction was not ethical.

I have been discussing two issues: customer satisfaction and ethical transactions. They are certainly not the same, but there is an overlap. Customers can be satisfied even if the transaction is unethical because the buyer does not have all the information that the seller has. The customer has not been told all the details. Customers can also be dissatisfied even if the transaction passes the ethical screen.

Over the long run, however, the two concepts converge; customer satisfaction and ethical transactions tend to go hand in hand. Although customers enjoy being fooled by magicians—they are willing to suspend their disbelief—they do not like being fooled by sellers in day-to-day marketplace transactions.

In the customer's mind, fairness demands both the absence of trickery and a sense that the customer has benefited from the transaction as much as the seller. This is at least a good beginning in the search for the definition of a fair price.

1. What methods do economists use to determine the fair price of a product?

2. Do you agree that the service station example was an ethical transaction and Amazon's free shipping offer was not?

Is That Your Final Offer?

Bargaining, negotiating, or haggling over prices is not an everyday activity for most people in the United States. In their ordinary purchasing of goods and services, people seldom question the marked or quoted price. To be sure, there are exceptions. The prices set on most new and used automobiles are for the most part still open to negotiation. In the real estate market, prices of homes and sometimes even rental units are normally set higher than what sellers expect to receive because they know they'll need to bargain with prospective buyers. However, on their daily ventures to Macy's, Kroger, or even the corner specialty store, people buy or do not buy at the marked price without questioning it.

Such is not the case universally, and I was reminded of this recently on my first trip to Beijing, China. A trusty guidebook had warned me that bargaining over prices was expected and customary in Beijing, and I accepted this advice with a mixture of worry and excitement. Would I be up to the challenge?

Almost immediately upon my arrival, I was initiated into this unfamiliar experience. As I browsed through a major department store in one of the city's more affluent (read: tourist) districts, each time I stopped to examine or even remark on a particular item, the salesperson would produce a calculator and reduce the marked price by 10% "for me." Sincere interest and extended bargaining almost always resulted in larger discounts.

In smaller shops, I found that the reductions offered from the marked prices were even greater; they usually started at 30%. I had the ultimate bargaining experience with vendors at the souvenir and postcard stalls that surround the entrance to the Great Wall. These seasoned traders were reluctant ever to say no to a potential sale, and if their proffered discounts were rebuffed, they would invariably ask me what I was willing to pay.

Some days later, as I reminisced about my buying experiences in a society and an economy so different from the United States, I tried to consider the practice of bargaining over prices from a marketing ethics perspective. Because the concept of a fixed price is so engrained in my mind, I assume that two buyers of the same merchandise, at the same time and place, and under the same circumstances ought to be treated the same—that is, be quoted the same price—by the seller. Would it be fair if one of the buyers was required to pay a higher price?

Using utilitarianism as my framework of analysis, I examined both the immediate and the long-term aspects of the question. It strikes me that the disadvantage, or cost, to one of the buyers is offset by the advantage, or benefit, to the other buyer. Alternatively, any cost to the buyer is off-set by a benefit to the seller. Predictably, it is more difficult to weigh the long-term costs and benefits. Does the prevalence of bargaining and haggling over prices lead to a lack of trust and confidence in the system? Does this cause diminished economic activity, which would penalize everyone? As always, it is difficult at best to assign values in such a utilitarian analysis, and it is impossible to be certain that the effects of the alternatives on all individuals or groups have been considered.

So I turned to deontology as an analytical framework and asked myself whether the practice of haggling over prices, which inevitably results in some buyers paying more than others, is *fair* and *just*. To satisfy those requirements, fairness and justice, both buyers and sellers must have, more or less, equal knowledge about the product. This equilibrium is known as "perfect knowledge." It happens that perfect knowledge is also an axiom in microeconomic theory. Of course, it was easier in the days of Adam Smith for both buyer and seller to assess the value of a pair of gloves, to use one of Smith's examples, than it is today for the buyer to assess the value of a computer (What really is inside that gray box?), an over-the-counter pain reliever, or even a can of pasta sauce from the supermarket. Invariably, sellers know quite intimately what they are selling, whereas because of the complexities of many of the goods and services being sold today, buyers have a difficult, if not impossible, task of finding out the ingredients or components of a prospective purchase and making an informed judgment about its value. During my shopping trips to various stores in Beijing, I could not be certain if the Casio wristwatch I was contemplating was a genuine article or a fake, whether the necklace of lovely green beads was true jade or a less valuable jadite, or whether the small stone figure was truly a hand-carved antique, as labeled, or something that had come off an assembly line only a few days earlier.

Buyers and sellers must have a mutual understanding about the product. Beyond that, they must also have a mutual understanding about the buying *process* if justice and fairness are to prevail. In the United States, both employees and customers of supermarkets understand that the shelf price on a quart of milk is fixed and not subject to bargaining. But what about the Beijing jewelry store owner and the perhaps unwary foreign customer? What if the foreigner assumes that the marked price of an item is fixed, whereas the shopkeeper has anticipated a bargaining process and has set the price much higher because of this? Is this a just and fair transaction? I asked colleagues from both China and India who confirmed that some bargaining over price is a normal and expected part of the buying process for them, and so they are not at a disadvantage relative to the seller. Is it ethical, however, to take advantage of a foreigner by offering a 10% discount when the seller really expects to sell the item at a 30% discount? Does the seller's superior understanding of the buying process give him or her a built-in advantage and thus doom the chances for an equitable and ethical transaction?

My conclusion? A fixed, one-price system is not an absolute requirement for an ethical transaction between buyer and seller. There is nothing inherently wrong with haggling and bargaining over price *if* both parties understand and agree on the "rules of the game." The problem arises when one or the other party—invariably the buyer—is less informed and does not understand what the rules of the game really are. Although we may not be inclined to pity the inept or unaware Western tourist who buys souvenirs from the wily vendors at the Great Wall, the principle remains the same: Fairness requires at least a close approximation to perfect knowledge—that buyers and sellers have a roughly equal understanding of both the product or service under consideration and the purchasing process.

1. Why do U.S. consumers tolerate price negotiations for car and home buying but accept set prices on most other goods and services?

2. Using the utilitarian framework, analyze price bargaining between buyer and seller.

3. How would you assess the fairness or justice of a transaction that is based on price bargaining?

When Is a Sale Not a Sale?

There was a time when the biggest selling day of the year for most department and specialty stores was the day after Christmas. Retailers would mark down all their seasonal merchandise on that day, and they would begin their traditional white sales and sales on Christmas cards, Christmas ornaments, and intimate apparel. Customers knew they would find bargains in the stores beginning the 26th of December, so the stores were jammed.

Holding off clearance sales until after Christmas is now only a relic of the past. The beginning of the end came innocently enough. A disappointing season led some stores to start the after-Christmas sales a few days early to get the jump on their competitors and take advantage of the pre-Christmas crowds. The next year the stores had to repeat the pattern to make their projected sales figures. And so it went. Each year there was additional pressure to break the sale a few days or a week earlier. Now the promotions start before Thanksgiving and continue through January to bolster the end of the retail year.

What we have experienced is creeping sales promotions to go along with the creeping Christmas decorations and the creeping catalogs. There really was a time when Christmas decorations were not put up until the day after Thanksgiving, and Christmas catalogs were mailed at about the same time. We can bemoan the current situation and long for the good old days, and we can even question whether the current pattern makes good business sense.

However, we must also look for a moral dimension in this new marketing pattern. Are there ethical issues at stake here? What merchandise are the stores putting on sale? What sort of markups are they taking? What kind of markdowns? How are the stores describing the prices to their customers? When is a sale not really a sale?

In this new pattern of merchandising, stores have learned that they must buy for their pre-Christmas promotions. To have enough inventory to make their projected sales figures, they cannot rely solely on marking down their regular merchandise. The merchandising of these sales has become an important part of the stores' seasonal planning, and it opens the door to the possibility of unethical pricing and promotion.

Let's say a store is selling women's cashmere turtleneck sweaters imported from Scotland. The store buys them for $87.50 and sells them for $200. Now, suppose it wants to have enough sweaters for sale before and after Christmas and to supplement its current stock. Sometime during the fall selling season, the store buys the knitter's remaining inventory for $45 each, adds them to the current stock, and runs a sale at $119 or even $99. The store tells its customers that these sweaters are "regularly" $200.

Any ethical problems? No, not really. The sweaters that have been added to the sale assortment are the same as those the store sold for $200. The merchandising problem is that the assortment, even with the addition of the knitter's remaining inventory, may not be good enough. To prepare for this possibility, the store works the sale into its merchandising plan from the very beginning. As early as the previous February, the store plans for a second shipment of the sweaters in November—all the best colors and in the proper sizes—and perhaps the store can negotiate a price of only $70 per sweater on this late-season delivery. Now the store is guaranteed to have a good assortment and the necessary quantity of sweaters for the sale, even though the resulting gross margin percentage will suffer.

Still no ethical problem, even when the store tells its customers that the sweaters are regularly $200. Again, the second shipment may not have been in stock at that price, but they are exactly the same as the sweaters that were.

What if the knitter is unwilling or unable to supply this late shipment of sweaters at this lower price? The store then may turn to a secondary supplier, say, an importer of cashmere sweaters from Hong Kong. These sweaters are almost as good as the Scottish ones. Although Scottish cashmere is widely considered the best in the world, Chinese cashmere is respectable. The sweaters from Hong Kong may be cut-and-sewn garments instead of fully fashioned. Perhaps the roll of the turtleneck is not quite as long, the sweater is half an inch shorter, and it is of lesser weight than the Scottish ones but with only slight differences that most customers would never notice. The store can buy these sweaters in the proper size and color assortment for only $52.50 each.

Now the store can put these new sweaters together with the original cashmeres and have a great selection for the sale, a good price, and a good markup. Any ethical problems now? That depends on how the store describes this sale and these sweaters to its customers. Does it claim that all the sweaters on sale regularly sell for $200? Does the store put $200 price tickets on the Hong Kong sweaters and then show a markdown to $119? It would be difficult and clumsy to describe the Hong Kong sweaters as "comparable to" those from Scotland, but more important, it isn't true.

Too much deceit in the use of comparative prices has led to regulations in many states. But, beyond legal restrictions governing what merchants tell or don't tell their customers in their ads and signs, what is the implicit message to customers when the store mixes the two groups of sweaters together? Doesn't the merchant hope that the customer will assume that the sweaters are all alike and that the two groups are of equal value?

Merchants need to be honest in their use of comparative pricing, and they must be careful in their merchandising so that they offer their customers honest value. Playing games with prices and with merchandise that is almost the same may help them make their figures for any one season. Over the long run, however, their reputations and goodwill with their customers will suffer. Customers will be angry about comparative prices they perceive to be phony, and they will feel patronized by retailers they thought they could trust. This game of playing fast and loose with prices may prove a winner for the retailer over the short run. Over the long run, it will always be a losing proposition.

1. Under the circumstances described previously, is it unethical for the store to mix the two groups of sweaters together and price them all the same, even though the country of origin is shown clearly on the label of each sweater?

2. Is there some proper or ethical markup percentage beyond which a store should not go?

14

Marketing as a Zero-Sum Game

At the heart of the buyer–seller relationship in consumer goods marketing, there is a certain tension that troubles the ethicist. The exchange process for the buyer is, to be honest, often a zero-sum game. If the seller, either the manufacturer or the retailer, is able to extract better terms, it benefits to the detriment of the buyer. Conversely, if the buyer negotiates a better price, then his or her benefit is increased at a cost to the seller. Unlike ethicists, economists view every transaction as a win–win situation; both buyer and seller must gain something from each exchange.

These two points of view seem antithetical, but they are not mutually exclusive. The economist looks at supply and demand curves, noting the areas of surplus that accrue more to buyers if the price is relatively low or more to sellers if the price is relatively high. The ethicist focuses on the buyers and sellers as individuals rather than as groups and is concerned about fairness. It is not enough for the ethicist that both buyer and seller benefit from the transaction. If the seller's benefit is consistently and significantly greater than the buyer's, then the exchanges may be unjust.

The economist ignores these qualitative factors, and with good reason. Barring some element of force or extortion, both buyer and seller must benefit to some degree from every transaction, or one or the other would refuse to participate. Even in the face of this rational, quantitative approach, however, the ethicist should not be ignored. If too much of the surplus goes to either the buyer or the seller, justice is not served. And what about the individual buyers who are forced out of the market as the price moves higher?

Business executives do not make marketing decisions on the basis of these esoteric views. It is quite clear to the marketer that making a sale at a higher price, other things being equal, means a higher profit. If the price can be held constant while the quality of the product is decreased—

15

The Ethics of ATM Fees

It is hard to remember a time before automated teller machines (ATMs). They are one of those technological advances that have proved so useful and convenient that they have quietly assumed a vital place in our daily lives. Now it would be hard to imagine getting along without them. Quite naturally, there is a price to pay for such convenience, and it comes in the form of charges that most banks impose on their customers when they use other banks' ATMs. These charges are the subject of some controversy.

Not long ago, a major daily newspaper delved into the issue. In effect, some bank customers are not concerned about the charges and believe that the convenience is worth the relatively small fee. I have read of one woman who nonchalantly accepted a $1.50 charge at a nearby ATM to withdraw $20 from her account, even though she could have avoided the charge by walking a block farther to her own bank's ATM.

Several consumer advocacy organizations, however, have a less sanguine perspective on these escalating fees. They do the arithmetic and point out that the woman paid 7.5% for the privilege of accessing her own money. They denounce the fees as unwarranted and unreasonable, and they claim that bank customers do not understand them. The implication is that the banks are involved in a covert form of price gouging and that such practices are unethical.

I disagree. I am not convinced that the fees themselves are unethical, though I do have some reservations about how customers are informed about them. Don't misunderstand me. I dislike paying transaction fees, and I will happily walk or drive out of my way to avoid them. I have probably used more than $1.50 worth of gasoline to avoid the bank charge, which perhaps makes my actions even less rational. In any case, I do not believe that these bank fees qualify as price gouging. Let's sift through some considerations of this matter.

It is no secret that it is far less expensive for a bank to handle a typical deposit or withdrawal transaction through an ATM than a live teller. The newspaper article cited a differential of roughly four times: $.27 for the ATM versus $1.07 for the live teller. Given these figures, it would make more sense for the banks to charge a fee for the privilege of using a teller behind the counter. In fact, a few banks tried this, but customers reacted so adversely that the banks quickly retreated, at least temporarily. Customers have been slow to accept the concept of paying to get their own money out of the bank using the services of a teller, which had always been available free of charge.

Banks have discovered that most customers do not object to the nominally modest charges for using other banks' ATMs. Remember that though the ATMs do indeed save banks money by reducing the number of live tellers, the machines are expensive to install, more than $50,000 each. As banks compete with one another by making more of their own machines available to their customers in more convenient locations, the cost of this competitive strategy increases dramatically. One industry expert said that he doubted whether banks made any money at all on ATM charges.

It is also true that businesses of all sorts are examining their expense structures with a fine-tooth comb, weeding out unnecessary costs and charging for hitherto free services if they can do so and remain competitive. Banks are no exception. A bank's profitability depends largely on the difference between the interest rate it charges on home and business loans and the interest rate it pays on the money it uses or borrows. As these short-term and long-term rates fluctuate, a bank's profits will wax and wane beyond its control, so it is not surprising or unreasonable for a bank to search for alternative sources of revenue to help offset its expenses.

If customers choose to pay the $1.50 ATM fee for the convenience of not walking an extra block, that certainly is their prerogative. Yes, 7.5% seems like an outrageous amount to pay to access one's own money, but a customer who withdraws $200 instead of only $20 pays a fee of less than 1%. Moreover, it is entirely appropriate for the consumer advocacy groups to alert bank customers of these sometimes hidden ATM charges.

There's the rub: Are these fees really hidden? Because if they are, then the practice is indeed unethical, and the banks should be castigated. Last week, I received my monthly statement from my bank and with it an insert with the bold headline "Important Notice." The rest of the flyer was in small print. Normally, I throw these away without so much as a glance. This time, however, I glanced at it long enough to read that the ATM fee for using another bank's ATM would soon go from $1.50 to $2.00.

Well, the bank did not go out of its way to make this 33% increase in its fee obvious, but I cannot claim that the news was hidden. If I opt for the convenience of throwing the insert away to avoid the fine print, there is a cost for that convenience. And these are not major sums. At other times, I have criticized banks for being less than forthcoming about their charges on credit cards, but those charges can amount to hundreds and sometimes even thousands of dollars. How much more notification would we require of a bank for these $1.50 or even $2.00 charges?

In summary, here we have the odd situation of most banks charging a fee for a newer, less expensive service while continuing to offer the old-fashioned, more expensive service of live tellers for free. Although this may not make much business sense, at least not on the surface, it hardly qualifies as an ethical infraction. Consumers must have the right to decide for themselves how much any specific convenience is worth, as long as they know the cost of the convenience and are not hoodwinked in any way.

And yes, the amount of the fee in question does have a bearing. A more expensive charge would require more effort on the bank's part to act responsibly and make sure its customers are properly informed. In this case, I am willing to give the banks the benefit of the doubt; the advance notice they gave me in the fine print is adequate for an occasional charge of $1.50.

1. Is it unethical for banks to charge for the less expensive ATM service if they offer the traditional teller service free of charge?

2. In analyzing the ethics of this or any issue, does the amount of money involved—in this case, $1.50—make a difference? Or is it that a principle is at stake and needs to be defended?

16

In Search of Fair Prices

In the late 1990s, a little-known Minnesota company, Green Tree Financial, provided mortgage financing for mobile homes and prefabricated houses. The company dominated this small niche of the market to such an extent that critics complained that its interest rates (i.e., the prices the company charges for its financing services) were too high and, indeed, unfair. The company responded that its interest rates were in line with the market.

In line with the market. Is that sufficient to ensure that prices are fair? In an open, capitalist system with a free and competitive market, prices are determined by the interactions of buyers who are seeking the best prices they can find and sellers who are trying to attract these buyers. Presumably, a buyer and a seller must agree on a price or there would be no transaction; again, does this ensure that the price is fair and passes the ethical screen?

For the sake of carrying on this analysis, let's assume that the Minnesota company is not acting illegally and that its domination of the market is not the result of anticompetitive activity. In other words, other lenders are free to enter this market if they believe they can make a profit. Under these conditions, if the Minnesota company were weighing the interest rates against the risks involved and charging above-market prices, competitors could enter the market and drive the interest rates down.

This economic theory is straight from the pages of Adam Smith, who was writing more than 200 years ago. And therein lies the problem: In Smith's model, buyer and seller come together in a market in which neither could dominate the other. Not only were other buyers and sellers providing competition on both sides of the transaction and therefore keeping prices low through the workings of the "invisible hand," but there was also what contemporary economists call "perfect knowledge." For the market to function properly, both buyer and seller must have roughly equivalent knowledge of the product to make a truly rational decision about whether to pursue the transaction.

The product (or, rather, the service) in question is mortgage financing for mobile homes. Real estate mortgages of any kind are bewildering contracts that involve a complex mixture of fixed or variable interest rates, down payments, length or term of the loan, points, recording fees, title search costs, and balloon payments. It would be a surprise if the buyer of the mobile home really understood the terms, including all the fine print, especially as the buyer is unlikely to enter this market more than once or twice in a lifetime.

Let's look at groceries as another example. Can consumers understand even the products they buy regularly well enough to decide if the price is fair? Take a trip through your favorite supermarket and note how many products are labeled "lite." What exactly does this mean, and how important is it to the buyer's health? How should the buyer interpret this partial list of ingredients on a package of soup: autolyzed yeast extract, guar gum, xanthan gum, hydrolyzed wheat gluten, sodium erythorbate, and so on?

If consumers have difficulty understanding a simple product such as a cup of soup, what happens when consumers must make decisions about an automobile, a computer, or a wireless telephone? If they are unlikely to understand fully the product under consideration, how can they judge whether the price is fair? Marketers would argue that at this point, brand names become important, and this is true. Under these circumstances, consumers will often choose a brand that is familiar. But does that not beg the question of fairness? Just because the brand has been on the market for decades and the manufacturer has invested millions of dollars promoting the brand, it is not necessarily true that the intrinsic value of the branded product is worth more than a much newer, less familiar brand. So, a well-known brand name does not guarantee a fair price.

Nowhere is the search for fair prices more difficult than in the health care industry. Insurance companies, more often than not, pay the bills, so they must have a role in deciding whether a pharmaceutical company's price is acceptable and fair. But will the insurance company make that decision in the interest of the patient or its own bottom line? Physicians take an oath that they will act in the best interests of their patients, but they are under great pressure from managed health care organizations to avoid costly medications. Pharmacists can play a key role by recommending lower-priced generic drugs rather than higher-priced brands, but they too are influenced by their own profit considerations.

Patients, as the end users, are arguably the least knowledgeable participants in this enormously complex marketing process. Should a patient be expected to judge whether an early dose of Genentech's tissue plasminogen activator (TPA) is really worth the original price of $2,500 per dose? Tests show that when taking this medication, the patient's chances of surviving a heart attack is increased 10%–20%. Is this a fair price?

Was Burroughs Wellcome's original price for AZT, $10,000–$12,000 for one year's dosage, fair? It would extend the life and ease the suffering of an AIDS patient. At that price, however, only a fraction of the HIV/AIDS community in the United States could afford the treatment, and practically no one could in Africa, where the disease has hit the hardest. Burroughs Wellcome argued that the price was reasonable and enabled the company to recoup its enormous investment costs, but it subsequently lowered the price under continued public pressure. What is a fair price for such a product?

A free market is the most efficient economic system, but it does not follow that society will consider all prices that markets establish, whether for mobile home mortgages or exotic prescription drugs, fair. A critical goal must be to strengthen the consumers' bargaining position so that they can make better and fairer decisions. This can be achieved by government-mandated regulation of manufacturers and retailers, government-mandated consumer education, growth and strengthening of consumer advocacy groups, and the self-restraint of sellers. For all kinds of reasons, the last alternative is the most attractive, but its track record is not good. In the ongoing struggle between economics and ethics and between short-term and long-term strategies, too seldom does ethics prevail. Perhaps more of a focus on the moral dimension of marketing will help even the score.

1. For which of the products and services you buy is it the most difficult for you to judge whether the price is fair?

2. If buyers are unable to fully comprehend the value of a product, what then are the sellers' responsibilities?

PROMOTION AND ADVERTISING

Introduction

Of the traditional four P's of marketing, promotion is questioned the most often in discussions of ethical behavior. There seems to be an inescapable pull and tug between the buyer, who wants complete and factual information about the product, and the seller, who wants to paint the product in the most compelling light.

Honesty is one of the most basic principles of every ethical system across time and cultures. Therefore, dishonest advertising is easily dealt with from an ethical perspective. Telling outright lies in the advertising and promotion of a product is clearly unethical as well as illegal. Making patently false claims about products or about the conditions of sale is simply not debatable. *Dishonesty* is wrong. However, there are three categories of ethical questions pertaining to *honesty* and promotion that cannot be so easily resolved: How much puffery should be allowed, how much of the truth must be told, and who should distinguish between tasteful and distasteful advertising.

Puffery

Puffery is as old as promotion itself. It stems from the seller's economic imperative to make the sale and close the deal. The seller's natural desire is to convince the buyer that the product will not only satisfy the buyer's needs but also do so quicker and more completely than any competing product.

How often does a retailer proclaim in an ad, "Sale of the Year" or even "Sale of the Century"? Claims such as "Lowest Price Ever" or "Limited Time Only" are commonplace. Superlatives are bandied about constantly: fastest, most powerful, tastiest, best value, and so on. Consumers become so inured to such claims that they seldom stop to question whether those claims are true. In practice, the seller has the right to exaggerate, but there are no clear guidelines as to how far this right may be pushed.

The Whole Truth

In testifying before a court of law, witnesses swear to tell "the whole truth." But what is required of marketers? Should an airline, for example, tell its potential customers that it has a poor on-time arrival record? Should manufacturers of chain saws or inline skates be required to tell purchasers how many fatal or serious accidents have resulted from the use of those products? Should fast-food restaurants warn customers about the dangers of a high-fat or high-sodium diet? None of these is required by law.

Sellers of food, beverage, and personal-care products are required to tell consumers all of the ingredients that go into those products, including all of the chemical additives to enhance the flavor or the color. It is not at all clear, however, how much consumers actually benefit from such regulatory requirements. Do they actually read those labels, and even if they do, can they understand whether expeller-pressed sesame oil will help or hurt them, whether 330 milligrams of sodium in a serving of barbecue sauce is a lot or a little, or what in the world calcium disodium EDTA really is?

"Taste" in Advertisements

From time to time, everyone is confronted with an ad that is tasteless. For some, tasteless may be the use of explicitly sexual messages to promote a product. For others, it may be poking fun at various segments of the population: racial groups, women, the less educated or less sophisticated, the disabled, the elderly. For others still, it may be the promotion of values they consider harmful: messages that imply that they can be fulfilled only if they drive a more expensive car, wear designer clothes, or live in a gated community.

Although it may be wrong—that is, unethical—to seriously offend viewers or readers of ads, it is not at all clear who will be the arbiter of good taste. There is no question that the U.S. population is more prudish than its French counterpart when it comes to the acceptance of female nudity in advertising. Yet citizens of Japan would find many U.S. ads offensive. In the United States, sexual images in ads that would never have been used 25 years ago are now acceptable. There are references and symbols regarding racial or ethnic groups, for example, that were used freely 40 years ago but are not used today because they would be considered offensive. Standards regarding what is or what is not offensive are not static but are constantly changing.

The challenge, therefore, is for marketers to draw the boundary between good and bad, right and wrong, and acceptable or unacceptable in the content of their promotional messages. Too often, marketers are faced with the same old tension between economics and ethics. There is the temptation to exaggerate claims about products, to conceal any information about unsafe or unhealthy products, and to push the limits of sexual content in ads to ensure that they are noticed among all the other competing messages—all in the name of increasing profits.

At some point, this tension creates a gap between organizational performance and societal expectations. In other words, some marketers create ads and promote products and services in ways that are unacceptable to significant segments of society. This is the gap referred to in the introduction to this book. As noted there, the gap will be closed by government intervention if marketers do not exercise restraint—that is, if marketers do not close the gap themselves by bringing their ads and their activities into line with what is socially and culturally acceptable.

The following essays explore a variety of moral issues related to advertising and other forms of promotion.

17

The Marketing of "Hope"

In 1998, an advertising supplement appeared in *The Washington Post* titled, "Transformations, Cosmetic Surgery." On the cover was a full-color shot of a beautiful young woman enjoying the sun beside a swimming pool—the picture of health and happiness. Inside, the supplement was a rather extraordinary collection of advertising, and some editorial copy, too, for a wide array of products and procedures to improve the hand that Mother Nature has dealt us.

A little too much fat around the stomach? Try abdominoplasty, better known as a tummy tuck. Aimed at men: Too little hair? Various remedies are offered, from microsurgical transplants to a once-a-day pill that was recently cleared by the Food and Drug Administration. Aimed at women: Too much hair on legs, face, or underarms? Eliminate it with electrolysis, laser treatments, or chemical techniques. Aimed at both sexes: facelifts, eyelid lifts, chin and cheek "improvements," nose reshaping, and treatments for varicose veins. Another ad promoted penile enlargement and lengthening. Several ads suggested breast enhancement, breast lifting, and tumescent liposuction for women. Endoscopic surgery, collagen treatments, and sclerotherapy were offered to those who know what the words mean. More mundane ads featured weight-loss methods, permanent makeup clinics, and more dazzling smiles through a variety of dental treatments. This is a brave new world.

Scanning this supplement through a marketing ethics lens yields many different conclusions. At one end of the spectrum is the view that this advertising is doing exactly what textbooks say advertising is meant to do: inform potential customers about new products and services and where they can get them. This is a field, like any other in medicine, that is driven by new technologies appearing at least every month. Producers and service providers must use advertising to let customers know what is available. At the other end of the spectrum is the darker perspective that readers of the paper are being manipulated and treated like fools. Do people really believe the promises some of these ads make?

Somewhere in the middle of the spectrum there are questions about values. Do marketers promote too heavily the idea that happiness depends on having a more perfect, more youthful body? Are marketers playing too much on people's vanity, self-doubt, and insecurity? Is their goal to uncover another segment of "vulnerable" customers: men and women so insecure about their physical appearance that they will gladly pay hundreds or thousands of dollars for results they admit are risky and, quite likely, short-term?

Playing on the insecurity of customers is hardly new. Remember the door-to-door vacuum salesman who warned the housewife about what her guests might think if her carpets looked dingy, or the encyclopedia salesman who urged parents not to neglect the education of their children?

Because I have been mostly bald for many years, my attention went quickly to some of the hair loss ads in the *Post* supplement. Perhaps I have been luckier than most in my situation, because I have been able to lead a normal, active, and happy life over the years. But that is not what people would expect from reading some of the copy. Instead, I learned that "diminishing hair means sinking self-esteem, loss of quality of life, and even depression. [Hair loss] can be like a constant, pervasive reminder of your impending death" (p. 5). That is scary stuff! No wonder business in the hair loss industry now totals $1.5 billion.

I believe that most of the material in this supplement is ethical; that is, it is not unethical. However, I do have concerns, and they fall into two general categories. The first is the special responsibility of health care professionals in dealing with their patients/customers. Almost all the ads in this supplement, and much of the editorial copy as well, were written by or for medical doctors. In the doctor–patient relationship, there is a wide information gap—what economists call an asymmetrical situation. Because patients/buyers have so little technical knowledge of the healing arts and new technologies, they must rely almost entirely on the doctor's/seller's knowledge as well as trust that the seller will not take advantage of them. When "before-and-after" photos are used to promote tummy tucks or hair loss treatments, they should be accompanied by prominent disclaimers, probability estimates, and warnings of potential risks. The ads and editorial copy in this supplement were uneven at best in how well they met this standard.

The second general category of problems regards marketers building false expectations. Yes, these are adults who will read supplements such as this, and yes, this type of promotion has been going on for a long time. Charles Revson, founder of Revlon, is often quoted as saying that his company really was in the business of "selling hope." One of the ads in the supplement promises "A New You for the New Millennium" and shows a butterfly emerging from a drab cocoon. It holds out the hope for the reader of a "transformation from the ordinary caterpillar to a creature of grace, elegance, and beauty. We can help you to become like a Butterfly" (p. 10).

Nevertheless, there is something a bit sad, and maybe even dangerous, about searching out insecure men and women and offering them the promise of a more romantic, vigorous, fulfilling life if only they can get to the bottom of a bottle of pills or spend enough money for a surgical procedure that may turn out to be neither brief nor painless. The fine print in one of the ads boasts, "The results of this procedure appear to produce less swelling, bleeding, and bruising than ever before.... The patient is usually able to walk around the day after the operation."

The marketing of health care in general is fraught with problems. Especially problematic is the marketing of cosmetic surgery, hair loss treatments, and other medical "cures" that are for the most part elective. Most of the material in this particular advertising supplement may not have crossed the ethics boundary, but it is certainly flirting with the edge. Physicians have not only the right but also the obligation to promote their services and new technologies. But blending the health care skills and the healing arts with the blandishments of a circus huckster, or even of Charles Revson, is a troublesome mixture. As physicians turn themselves into marketers, they must be especially conscious of ethical pitfalls.

P.T. Barnum may well have been right that every minute produces another "sucker," but the moral question is how marketers react to this. Do they take advantage of the newly created psychographic segment of insecure, aging adults? Or do they treat these customers with care and respect, using appropriate disclaimers and avoiding the temptation of overselling to this vulnerable group?

We return to the question: Is marketing a cooperative or an adversarial relationship?

1. What are the moral issues inherent in the promises made by the marketers of cosmetic surgery? Give examples.

2. What is the asymmetrical relationship between the buyer/patient and the seller/physician, and what moral problems does it suggest?

3. How can health care marketers balance educational content, which is often dull, and speculative content, which is exciting?

4. Under what circumstances is it ethical to market "hope"?

The Excesses of Puffery

18

Over the past several years, bottled water has become an important segment of the beverage industry. A youth- and health-oriented population that is obsessed with diet and exercise is no longer content with drinking water from a tap to quench its thirst. Some of the new products are simply pure water, albeit from attractive sounding sources such as mountain springs. Other products in this new wave of drinks, however, promise an extraordinary array of benefits that goes far beyond simply quenching thirst.

Recently, *The Wall Street Journal* reported that bottled-water marketers claimed that their new products, laced with vitamins and minerals, might do any or all of the following: burn off fat, suppress allergies, make the drinker feel stronger, help protect against cancer and heart disease, make the drinker feel sexier, and soothe the drinker's nerves.

These innovative beverages—some from Coke and Pepsi, some from small regional bottling firms—go well beyond the claims made by sports drinks such as Gatorade and Powerade to replenish nutrients. For example, Mo'Beta, from Odwalla, Inc., promises that its antioxidants and beta carotene will refresh "overworked cells" and guard against a host of medical problems, "even aging."

Raphah Inc.'s Vita-J "helps burn fat." Aloe'ha Beverage Corp. adds aloe vera to its carbonated drink to restore healthy skin and hair and create the "sparkle of youth." RJ Corr Naturals has introduced a ginseng soda with a dose of chromium that, a company spokesman claims, controls blood-sugar levels and may be associated with longer life spans.

Three thoughts come to mind. First, these claims conjure up such phrases as "snake oil," "elixir of youth," and "There's a sucker born every minute." We seem to be reliving the 1890s, and marketers are simply using fancy twenty-first–century chemical names and a pseudoscientific sophistication to appeal to the same old basic human hopes and dreams.

Second, these sorts of marketing claims focus our attention on the proper relationship among business, government, and overall society. For the better part of a century, we have heard the plea that government should "get off the back" of business. Under certain circumstances, however, it may be appropriate and necessary for government to intervene in the affairs of business with laws and regulations. It may be justified in this case for the Food and Drug Administration (FDA) to monitor the claims of these new bottled water drinks.

One justification for government intrusion into the buyer–seller relationship is that buyers have insufficient knowledge to judge sellers' claims about their products. These new "functional beverages" raise this concern. Customers may really believe the bottlers' claims for improved health and a longer life. Some of the drinks contain 1000% to 2000% of the recommended daily allowance of certain nutrients: vitamin C and beta carotene, for example. Furthermore, someone must draw the line between innocuous claims such as "supplying energy" and more medical-related promises such as improving metabolism, heartbeat, or cardiovascular rates.

Third, marketers must exercise some restraint. The question is not *whether* but *when*. At what point does lighthearted puffery end and cynical deception begin? If marketers stray too close to the latter, government regulators are sure to impose constraints that marketers are unwilling to adopt for themselves. Unfortunately, there are no clear guidelines or rules on this issue. The vague statements in the ethics code of the American Association of Advertising Agencies, for example, are of little help.

The temptation to move from simple puffery to unacceptable hyperbole is especially prevalent in a large, highly competitive industry such as soft drinks. The stakes are enormous. In a $50 billion industry, even a tiny improvement in market share can mean a big jump in profits. Unlike business-to-business marketing, in consumer goods marketing, buyers exercise no power whatsoever. There is no appreciable penalty for losing a few customers because of an overly aggressive marketing claim.

In an ideal world, marketers might turn to a business ethics textbook for guidance. Here, they would learn to use a utilitarian framework for analyzing the ethics of using unrestrained hyperbole in promoting a product. This would mean balancing the benefits and costs: measuring the benefits of greater sales and profits against the negative effects of consumers' unrealized expectations. Might not there be long-term problems as well: further erosion of public confidence in advertising and tighter regulations by the FDA and other government agencies?

The business ethics textbook would also require that the marketer question the rights of all the parties involved. Does not the seller have the right to free speech, including the right to say what it wants to say about its product, as long as the truth is not stretched beyond recognition? But doesn't the buyer have the right to be adequately informed about the product and the right *not* to be misled?

Sadly, such textbook analysis seldom reveals any clear and unequivocal solutions to ethical problems. The proper limits of puffery remain elusive. However, that does not mean that ethical analysis is worthless or that marketers can afford to ignore ethical issues. Having the courage to confront the issues and ask the questions is an important first step.

Marketers must rely less on puffery and more on the *factual* qualities of their products that make the products better, more rewarding, and healthier. Puffery is really too easy, too glib, and too superficial a solution for an advertising campaign. Marketers should require more from their advertising agencies or in-house executives.

Perhaps the time will come when we really can feel sexier, have a steadier heartbeat, refresh our overworked cells, burn off excess fat, and suppress allergies by drinking bottled water from the nearest convenience store. I fear that that time has not yet arrived. We, like Ponce de León, are still searching for the fountain of youth.

1. When do individual consumers need the protection of government agencies such as the FDA?

2. In the marketing of fortified bottled water drinks, how do we define and balance the rights of sellers and buyers?

19

Trust as a Necessary Ingredient

Trust, I fear, is something that marketers take for granted most of the time. They know it is a good thing, and they understand that it is probably connected to ethics in some way, but they certainly don't spend much time thinking about it. This is a mistake. They must not neglect or undervalue trust because it is so critical to a good relationship between buyer and seller. Yet too often, especially in advertising copy, marketers either stretch the truth too far or give their customers too little information and thereby dissipate whatever trust exists.

Trust has an uncomplicated meaning: confidence in the honesty and reliability of another. In the United States, the currency proclaims, "In God We Trust." But the oft used, humorous version of that slogan, "In God We Trust, All Others Pay Cash," is a reminder that in commercial dealings, trust may not be a sure thing.

Marketers should bear in mind that trust cuts two ways: Marketers want their customers to trust them, and they want to trust those that sell them products and services. They want radio and television stations to run their ads in the time slots for which they pay. If, as part of its sales pitch, an agency tells them that it will assign its most talented and creative people to their account, they want to be able to count on that. If one of their sales staff turns in a travel voucher, they want to believe that the amounts are valid. Undoubtedly, marketers will establish procedures to check these things occasionally, but their lives are smoother and their jobs simpler if they have trust in these matters.

Customers have similar hopes and expectations in their dealings with sellers. They want to be able to rely on products that are always what marketers say they are, prices that have no hidden gimmicks, and advertising that is honest.

Too often, however, marketers forfeit that trust. "Fifty Percent Off" mattress sales have been run so regularly for so long by so many retailers that few customers believe any longer that they are really buying a mattress for half of its real value. "Going Out of Business" sales have become so standard for oriental rug merchants that few people are surprised to see the same rug shop with the same banner at the same location month after month.

What do all the jokes about used-car salespeople imply but that they cannot be trusted? A few years ago, a major department store's close-out sale had barely begun before customers were complaining that some of the store's merchandise had been marked up before being put back out for sale under signs that read "30% Off Everything in the Store."

On a trip through Eastern Europe, where I had no knowledge of the languages, I was especially aware of the value of trust. In Budapest, the problem was particularly troublesome because the Hungarian language has no roots in common with the Latin, Greek, Germanic, or even Slavic tongues. Trust became an important factor in every simple transaction, and sometimes I was disappointed. Could I trust any taxi driver after one of them charged me twice the expected amount to go from the train station to my hotel? Did I trust (no, I did not) a young salesperson who tried to convince me that the porcelain I was considering was 120 years old? Could I really believe the sign in the shop window that was understandable, even in Hungarian: "Fonal Diskont"?

I had no trust whatsoever, thanks to a warning in a guidebook, that the promises made by street hustlers to give me a better exchange rate on my dollars for Hungarian forints were legitimate. My lack of trust seemed all the more justified when two would-be money changers, after buzzing about me on the crowded street for some time, were finally accosted and marched off by plainclothes policemen.

Nor did it help my trust in Hungarian coupons when I showed up at a nightclub with a coupon promising free admission only to be told that the slip was valid only during the daytime hours. Trust suffered another minor blow on my last day in Europe when my hotel did not have the promised free shuttle ride to the airport.

To preach the importance of trust and trustworthiness sounds so ... preachy. To advise that building trusting relationships between customers and marketing partners is not only good ethics but also good for long-term profits sounds so obvious. From time to time, however, it is useful for marketers to remind themselves and those who work for them that trust is a critical element in profitable business relationships. Marketers must remember too that it is their customers' perceptions, not their own, that are important. They may believe they are telling their customers all they need to know about their products, they may believe that their delivery promises are being kept, and they may believe that their advertising claims are straightforward, honest, and unambiguous, but do their customers share these beliefs?

Gone are the "good ol' days" when trust could be established by a simple handshake or a straightforward verbal assurance. Marketing relationships are now far too complex, too global, and too technological to rely on the old interactions between buyers and sellers. Now, the buyer must often rely on not just the seller but a third-party guarantor—for example, a government regulatory agency such as the Food and Drug Administration or a consumer advocacy group such as Consumer Reports.

It takes years and a large advertising budget dedicated to promoting the brand name to establish trust in a product. Yet that trust can be lost so quickly; witness the experiences of Firestone tires. Product recalls can restore lost trust if they are handled correctly and promptly. Johnson & Johnson went further than anyone expected in its recall of Tylenol several years ago, and the result was the reestablishment of trust in the brand beyond what the marketing world ever predicted. However, if a firm hesitates or resists the recall, as Firestone did, regaining trust is far more problematic.

If trust is such a precious commodity and is so easily dissipated, it would be a good idea for marketers to pay more attention to it. Trust can be measured, albeit it imperfectly and with some difficulty, through customer surveys and focus groups. Promotional messages can be tailored in ways that are designed to build up customers' trust in both a company and its products. What marketers cannot, or must not, do is take trust for granted.

1. What makes trust a necessary part of an ethical relationship between buyer and seller?

2. How is the possible short-term economic advantage of sacrificing trust balanced against the long-term problems that may result?

Manipulation and Virtual Reality

Virtual reality. It may be a contradiction in terms, but it is certainly a fascinating and increasingly important factor in our technologically oriented lives. And what an opportunity and challenge for marketers.

In 1999, a business commentator noted that we are entering a new era of marketing—in which the awesome power of the computer is harnessed to the age-old task of manipulating the consumer. Is that marketers' age-old task—manipulating the consumer? Or are advertisers just having fun, adding entertainment to the commercial side of television, creating illusions in exciting ways, capturing the consumer's attention with electronic tricks, and enhancing their products with digital sleight of hand?

Manipulation and its even more objectionable partner, deception, have appeared with distressing regularity. The medium of television, even without the aid of computer graphics, offers opportunities for tricks some advertisers cannot resist.

A few years ago, Colgate-Palmolive claimed lightheartedly that its Rapid Shave was such a superior shaving cream that it could actually help shave sandpaper. If that were true, what a wonderful job it would do helping shave a man's beard! To emphasize the message, the company's television ads showed a razor shaving the grit off sandpaper.

But wait. It wasn't really sandpaper that the agency used in the ad, but sand sprinkled on a sheet of glass. This provided a better visual effect. It also provided a reason for the Federal Trade Commission (FTC) to step in, rule that the ad was deceptive, and prohibit it from being aired.

A few years later, Campbell's created a television ad for its vegetable-beef stew that showed a steaming bowl fairly brimming over with chunks of vegetables and beef. It looked almost too good to be true. It was. Campbell's advertising agency needed a little help creating this appealing picture. It seems that when left to their own devices, the vegetable and beef chunks were rather uncooperative and sank to the bottom of the bowl. So the agency compensated by putting glass marbles in the bottom, which forced the chunks to the surface where they would be visible.

This, too, drew fire from the FTC. The commission ruled that the viewing public would expect the chunks to sink; therefore, seeing so many chunks, the public would be deceived into believing that Campbell's product had more vegetables and beef than it actually had. This ad also was stricken from the airwaves.

Where should the line be drawn between hyperbole and deception? Does every price billed as "the lowest of the year" really warrant that superlative? Does every ad for "the greatest sale of the year" need to be justified?

When it comes to an ad's visual effects, the sleek, powerful tiger that emerges from the automobile's gasoline tank is deemed acceptable, whereas an ad for Volvo, which alone among its peers withstands the weight of a truck on its roof (thanks to special, made-for-television supports), is not at all acceptable because the viewing public is likely to be misled.

We have cut our teeth on the fantasies of *Star Trek* and *The Matrix*, so what are the ground rules for advertising in the age of virtual reality? Now, whatever an advertising agency can imagine, a computer programmer can generate. So polar bears casually sip Coca-Cola, and in the dark of night the Statue of Liberty creakily glances at the Timex Indiglo watch glowing brightly on her wrist.

Should there be a new definition of deception? Are the FTC and the current guidelines up to the job? Are controls necessary at all, or is it possible to rely instead on the basic honesty of advertisers and the healthy skepticism and good sense of the viewing public? Unfortunately, the track record of advertisers and marketers is not good enough to warrant the removal of controls and the phasing out of a government watchdog, especially in an age in which, according to one commentator, computer drawing skills are playing on the imagination and fears of viewers in ways that were once reserved for fiction writers.

The proper, and profitable, course for advertisers and their computer-trained colleagues is to let their imaginations soar while avoiding deception. It is almost a cliché, but true nonetheless, that ads can be the most entertaining aspect of television programming. Advertisers should pursue creativity to the farthest dimension new technologies permit and in doing so capture the viewer's awe and attention. But they should treat those viewers as valuable customers rather than dupes. Tell them that what they just witnessed was a mirage or hoax, a miracle of modern technology. Let them understand the difference between reality and virtual reality.

If television viewers are valuable customers, they deserve to be courted and protected, not exploited. This requires adopting a long-range outlook rather than grabbing for a quick sale. More than anything else, it requires that marketers practice patience and restraint, two qualities that have been in short supply throughout marketing's history.

The alternative, however, is not a pleasant prospect. If marketers use computer-driven tools to deceive their customers for immediate profits, they will reap an ever larger, ever more controlling bureaucracy of regulators. That is the lesson marketing history teaches us. That is reality.

1. Give two examples of marketing creativity and/or marketing manipulation from your own experience of television or print advertising. Describe the differences.

2. What criteria should marketers use to guide the creative process and the use of computer-driven tools?

3. Do you believe consumers need government protection against manipulation? Explain using the examples in this essay.

21

Tobacco and the Limits of Public Relations

Marketing ethics concepts can be used to evaluate a firm's specific activities, or they can be a tool for analyzing the social impact of an entire industry over a period of time. This essay offers an example of the latter.

A few years ago, the tobacco industry—spurred on by both Republicans and Democrats in Congress—came close to reaching a comprehensive agreement regarding the marketing of cigarettes. However, the members of Congress and various anti-tobacco advocacy groups were too greedy. They insisted on such onerous terms that the industry withdrew from the discussions. At that point, in an attempt to explain itself to millions of skeptics and opponents and to salvage any remaining public goodwill, the tobacco industry launched a public relations program aimed at convincing the public that the industry had been poorly treated.

The strategy failed for a very simple reason: The tobacco industry had consistently squandered its legitimacy—had lost any trust and respect it may once have had—by its arrogance and insensitivity over the previous four decades. The industry's social acceptance and political capital evaporated, and it has only itself to blame. Consider the public image of the tobacco industry today in light of the following:

- ✦For more than 40 years, the industry refused to admit that there is a connection between smoking and a long list of deadly ailments, including lung cancer, in the face of overwhelming evidence.
- ✦The familiar photograph from several years ago shows seven chief executives of tobacco companies standing before a congressional committee raising their right hands and swearing that they do not believe nicotine to be addictive.
- ✦Until recently, tobacco companies were able to squash all product-liability challenges with their enormous power and practically unlimited legal resources and then boast about never paying a cent in damages.
- ✦In various trials in recent years, documents and internal memos have surfaced that show that the tobacco companies were conspiring to do exactly

92

what they had denied doing: suppress the link between cigarette smoking and cancer.

Given this recent history, is it any wonder the tobacco industry finds a hostile environment as it takes its case to the public and attempts to build grassroots support? A few years ago, in the face of mounting pressure in state capitols and city halls to restrict smoking in public places, the tobacco companies launched a similar campaign. They attempted to convince the public that its constitutional rights were in jeopardy. That campaign also went nowhere.

In the public debate over the marketing of cigarettes, the tobacco companies held their own as long as the issue under discussion was health consequences for adult smokers. As bad as those consequences are, the public did not want to prohibit consenting adults from smoking or even set more stringent marketing restrictions on adult-oriented promotion. Consumers, especially when they are warned by product labels, have the right to buy legal products even though the products may be harmful. But anti-tobacco advocates discovered the industry's Achilles' heel when the discussion turned to the effects of smoking on children. Indeed, the most effective anti-tobacco advocacy group during this period was a new organization, Campaign for Tobacco-Free Kids, that was financed with hundreds of thousands of dollars from various foundations and health organizations. With each discovery of secret documents showing the tobacco industry targeting teenagers, the industry found itself further entrenched in a public relations battle it could not win.

Even though the so-called comprehensive settlement failed, the tobacco companies agreed to settle the suits brought against them by states' attorneys general by eliminating some of their most pernicious marketing tactics and paying billions of dollars to the states to compensate for public health expenses caused by cigarette smoking in the past. At least some of those billions have paid for public health messages that are designed to keep teens from taking up the addiction.

Big Tobacco is not yet defenseless, however. It has two powerful aces up its sleeve. First, although the public is squarely behind the efforts of anti-tobacco forces to protect children, it does not favor banning cigarettes entirely and making smoking illegal even for adults. The specter of Prohibition in the 1920s still haunts the United States even today, and there are still 50 million to 60 million Americans who choose to smoke regardless of the consequences to their health.

Second, there is the cold reality of the economic power that the tobacco industry wields. To many, the industry may be an ugly duckling, but from an economic perspective, there is no denying that it is more like a goose that lays golden eggs. Tobacco farmers depend on the industry, cigarette companies employ thousands of workers directly, hundreds of thousands of wholesalers and retailers profit from the sale of cigarettes, and, of course, many politicians benefit from Big Tobacco's contributions. The principal debate is about how much gold from the goose finds its way into the tobacco companies' coffers versus how much is used to reimburse federal and state governments for the medical costs of smoking, to satisfy individual liability claims, and to fund anti-smoking public health programs. But no serious participant in the debate wants to kill the goose.

Controversy over tobacco marketing continues, both in the courts and in Congress, and the outcome is far from certain. What is certain, however, is that the industry faces an increasingly difficult public relations challenge. To face that challenge, for example, a tobacco company might introduce a cigarette with reduced levels of carcinogenic substances. Under different circumstances, this would be applauded as a step toward improved public health, but tobacco critics have responded that the new product may become an excuse for smokers not to give up their habit. When Philip Morris brags about launching a public relations program designed to limit cigarette purchases by preteens and underage teenagers at tobacco counters, the effort is immediately criticized. The focus shifts to the fact that the company's Marlboro brand is far and away the cigarette of choice among underage smokers. The industry's credibility, social acceptance, and legitimacy are waning. Under these conditions, the public is unlikely to become concerned about the industry's free speech rights, and even the cleverest public relations campaigns do not stand a chance.

1. For the tobacco industry, how has the short-term focus on economics, at the expense of ethics, led to serious long-term problems?

2. What is the connection between corporate public relations campaigns and the legitimacy of the firm or the industry?

Arrogance and Legitimacy

Arrogance is an unattractive characteristic. It conjures up a sense of superiority and elitism that rubs against the grain of our democratic ideals. It implies, at the very least, a lack of caring for and sensitivity to the concerns of others. Just as arrogance is unattractive in individuals, so too is it an inappropriate characteristic of corporations, and perhaps it is made even worse by the overwhelming power that corporations exercise in society. If corporations—indeed, entire industries and the business community overall—are to retain their legitimacy, that is, retain their positions as accepted, necessary, and integral parts of society, they must steer clear of arrogant actions and attitudes.

The pharmaceutical industry, for all the wondrous benefits it brings to people's lives, is often criticized for finding new ways to break the rules of ethical and perhaps legal behavior. For example, the marketing executives at Roche, the U.S. division of Swiss-based F. Hoffmann-La Roche, have discovered another novel way to circumvent those rules. They are thumbing their collective noses at the society in which they have the privilege to operate and, in the process, are showing a wanton disregard for the well-being of their customers, from whom they profit so handsomely. This is indeed arrogance.

In brief: the Food and Drug Administration (FDA) requires that a pharmaceutical company list all the potential side-effects that may result from taking or using a product when the company promotes the medical or health-related benefits of that product. This rule applies to prescription drugs advertised directly to consumers. Note that there are two conditions in this rule, and both are necessary to trigger the requirement for a sometimes lengthy list of side-effects: The advertisement must mention the product by name and also the purpose of the product—that is, what the product is meant to do.

Chris Adams (2001) of *The Wall Street Journal* reports that Roche has found a new way to get around this rule in recent television promotions of its weight-loss drug, Xenical: It has created not one but two commercials. The first commercial describes the medical problem, unhealthy weight gain, that the drug is intended to treat, but it never mentions the drug by name. The second one promotes Roche's brand name Xenical but does not mention the benefits. These ads are separated briefly in a television network's programming by unrelated advertising, but both use the same distinctive visual effects and the same music, so that viewers cannot help but make the connection between the brand name Xenical and weight loss. Presto! Alacazam! By sleight of hand, the rules have been circumvented, the company has promoted the product and the benefit without mentioning the potential side effects, and customer protection has been ignored. Another cadre of marketing executives at Roche and at Young & Rubicam, the agency that created the ads, feels smug that it has found one more loophole in the FDA regulations.

The *Journal* reports that this is the first example of such a scheme on television, though Schering-Plough has used similar tactics in a magazine advertisement for Claritin. It also reports that FDA officials said that they are exploring the Roche problem but believe that they have no legal remedy.

Let's examine this problem in a wider context. The pharmaceutical industry has been the subject of many of these essays, not because prescription drug marketers are less ethical than their counterparts in other industries, but because there are certain ethical problems that are unique to this industry. The nature of the products of this industry—in extreme examples, they may mean life or death—sets them apart from run-of-the-mill consumer goods. Also, consumers have no practical way to become knowledgeable about these products, so they cannot be expected to make informed decisions in the marketplace. Finally, marketing in this industry does not deal with a simple buyer–seller relationship or even a simple buyer–retailer–manufacturer relationship. The medical profession is deeply involved because doctors must recommend the drugs and write the prescriptions. The medical insurance industry is involved because insurance is often the ultimate payer. Pharmacists are involved because they are consultants, sometimes promoters of the product, and occasionally even advocates for the patients/consumers. These unique industry conditions create a thicket of potential ethical problems that is worthy of a subspecialty of business ethicists and of stand-alone graduate and undergraduate courses.

Add the relatively new practice of direct-to-consumer advertising, and the potential ethical problems are compounded. It was not without reason that the industry was prohibited for decades from advertising its prescription-only pharmaceutical products directly to the consuming public. The FDA believed that, among other problems, such advertising would create a strain between doctors and their patients. In any case, during the 1990s, the FDA relaxed the rules and made it feasible for pharmaceutical manufacturers to advertise to consumers as well as the medical profession, to establish their brand names, and to make potential customers aware that products treating their medical problems were available. The operative word here is "relaxed." The FDA certainly did not eliminate restrictions and conditions; the rule cited at the beginning of this essay is an example. But marketing executives at the pharmaceutical companies chafed at even these relaxed guidelines, and perhaps it was inevitable that one company (in this case, Roche) would find a way to get around them.

Those are the immediate problems. There are less direct, long-term implications as well. I have long questioned whether marketing, at its very core, is a cooperative or an adversarial activity. Sadly, tactics such as Roche's attempt to skirt FDA regulations seem to tip the balance toward the adversarial side. Certainly, Roche put itself in an adversarial position with the government. Lawyers at the FDA are exploring ways to show that Roche broke the law or, if Roche did not break the law, that more restrictive regulations are necessary.

More important, consider what such tactics reveal about the company's concern for its customers. This is such blatant flouting of the regulations that were, after all, established to protect these customers. The side effects Roche has taken such pains to hide from its customers can hardly be considered a mere technicality or a minor matter. In other advertising material, Roche tells potential Xenical users that "you may experience gas with oily discharge, increased bowel movements, an urgent need to have them, and an inability to control them." For Roche to find such a devious way to avoid revealing these potential problems shows an utter disdain for its customers' well-being, which is hardly an attitude we would like to find in a company that is supposedly devoted to the care and health of the public. It is an obvious example of a company using its superior power and knowledge to take advantage of consumers, opting for a short-term profit at the public's expense, and choosing economics over ethics.

I might be more forgiving of Roche were this the company's only transgression, but the *Journal* reports that Roche has been cited six times in four years for its weight-loss promotions. In another television commercial, for example, the company skirts the law by referring viewers to "our free, personalized support program, XeniCare" instead of mentioning the product name. Under pressure from the FDA, Roche agreed to change this ad.

For three or four decades, there has been a growing awareness not only among the critics of business but also among business leaders themselves that business has responsibilities beyond maximizing its profits for the benefit of its shareholders. It has responsibilities to a multitude of stakeholders, certainly including its customers and the government. Business as an institution must fit into and conform to the broader society of which it is such an integral part. Only then will society fully accept the business community and consider it a legitimate part of the whole. Arrogant tactics such as those by Roche are a significant step in the wrong direction. They damage the company's reputation and its various stakeholder relationships, and they cast a shadow over the pharmaceutical industry and the entire business community. They invite more draconian regulations by the government—the FDA has decided to review the whole subject of the direct-to-consumer advertising of prescription drugs—and they further contribute to the already existing suspicion that business in general cannot be trusted. In short, arrogance is not compatible with legitimacy.

1. What are the ethical problems unique to the pharmaceutical industry? Give examples.

2. Is it fair to say that drug manufacturers such as Roche and Schering-Plough tip the buyer–seller relationship from cooperative to adversarial? Give examples.

3. What are the probable consequences of arrogant tactics by even one segment of the business community?

23

When Does a Gift Become a Bribe?

The marketing of prescription drugs is the subject of ongoing attention from business ethicists, consumer activists, and government regulators. The interactions between drug companies' sales representatives and representatives of the medical profession are the most often scrutinized activities. The focus is on gifts and incentives and on the question: When does a gift become a bribe?

At the heart of marketing is the relationship between buyer and seller. In the prescription drug industry, however, that relationship is quite complex, and it differs significantly from other industries such as toothpaste or automobiles. Consider these three important differences:

◆ Buyers/patients and sellers/drug companies are not the only parties involved: Doctors, pharmacists, and insurance companies play critical roles as well. Because the choice of products is made by the doctor who prescribes them, drug companies aim much of their marketing strategies at doctors, who are technically intermediaries, rather than at the patients, who are the actual end users.

◆ Patients have little or no knowledge about the product, and this is unlikely to change because the product category is too technologically complex. They have no way to judge the value of one competing product over another, not to mention the health risks involved.

◆ Although toothpaste and automobiles represent varying degrees of importance to their purchasers, a prescription drug may mean the difference between life and death. Thus, health care marketing is unique.

Long ago, pharmaceutical companies realized that doctors are the key to success in their marketing strategies. In most cases, doctors play more than a simple consulting role because they are the only participant in the complex marketing process with knowledge of both the drug's benefits and properties and the patient's needs and medical condition. Although drug companies can now direct some of their marketing efforts directly at consumers, doctors are still their most important target.

The selling practice that has raised the most concern among ethicists and watchdog groups involves giving gifts to doctors. The danger is that a gift can become a bribe. Drug manufacturers give all sorts of things to doctors. They give them samples of their products, especially new products. How else can a doctor learn about the new drug's benefits and side effects and compare them with those of competing drugs? Few critics question the practice of giving samples, though there have been isolated cases of abuse.

Giving promotional items such as pens, pads, address books, and key rings is also common in the industry. This is acceptable to most ethicists, who assume that gifts of only modest value do not influence doctors' decisions.

Pharmaceutical representatives often provide meals for doctors and their staff. In this case, the value of the gift is far greater than a pen or a key ring, and it generates proportionately more ethical concern. Representatives and their companies defend the practice by arguing that it is often the only feasible way to get the doctor's time and attention, and in many cases, the doctor asks that the company host the meal as a convenience. However, there is at least a possibility that the free meal influences the doctor's choice of prescriptions.

Next on the ascending scale of questionable gifts is sending a doctor to conferences and seminars. Invariably, such conferences are held in attractive vacation spots—think of Palm Springs or Key West—and the time spent on actual business-related education, as opposed to time spent playing golf or tennis, is minimal. The line separating work from play, a learning experience from a boondoggle, becomes fuzzy. After being sent to a conference, the doctor may feel some real obligation to reciprocate by directing prescriptions to the company hosting the trip.

What is wrong with these practices? Why do ethicists and consumer activists find at least some of them unethical and unacceptable? Outright bribes are unethical in any industry, but the unique structure and circumstances of the pharmaceutical marketing situation make these practices especially suspect. Buyers and sellers are supposed to come together in the marketplace with somewhat equal standing, that is, equal knowledge of the product. Because that is impossible with prescription drugs, the patient *must* rely on the physician for professional advice. That advice must not be tainted by the incentives that are dangled in front of the doctor by drug manufacturers. It is absolutely imperative in this industry, given the possible life-and-death consequences, that patients be able to trust their physicians' prescription choices.

Five things are necessary to keep the system above reproach and maintain the public's confidence:

1. Drug makers must exercise restraint in their promotions and selling practices. If they take advantage of the unequal power they have in the marketing relationship with patients—because they have all the knowledge about the product and patients have little or none—they invite even more serious regulations than now exist.
2. Doctors must also exercise restraint and reject unreasonable incentives when they are proffered. This is easier said than done because almost every doctor would state, and perhaps actually believe, that the trip to Palm Springs did not really influence his or her choice of prescription drugs. Doctors must at all times act as the patient's counselor and advocate, not as a profit center.
3. Insurance companies must increase their oversight of doctors' prescription patterns, both to hold down costs and to ensure fairness.
4. Patients can help themselves by taking advantage of the increasing amount of information about prescription drugs that is available from advocacy groups such as Public Citizen and the American Association of Retired Persons (AARP).
5. Some degree of government regulation must continue. The government must be involved to ensure fairness in cases in which the buyer–seller relationship does not work perfectly and in which there is a more complex relationship such as when doctors act as intermediaries.

Although the public good can tolerate marketing practices that are ethically questionable in some industries, it cannot tolerate them in others. Prescription drugs fall into the latter category, and all parties to the marketing process in this critical industry—drug manufacturers, doctors, patients, insurance companies, and government regulators—must share in the responsibility of maintaining the highest level of ethical standards and preserving public confidence.

1. How does a bribe differ from what the government calls a "facilitating payment"?

2. What makes bribery questionable from an ethical perspective?

3. In what other industries do buyers have little or no knowledge about the product and are, therefore, at the mercy of the seller?

24

On the Marketing of Dinosaurs

In 2001, the Universal Studios movie, *Jurassic Park III*, hit theaters across the United States, and its wonders of creativity are not limited to the story line and the technological magic of animation. Universal's marketing department, not to be left behind, created a new format of newspaper advertising for the expected blockbuster film. According to *The Wall Street Journal*, the studio convinced many newspapers to run the shadow of pteranodon, the flying dinosaur reptile that has become something of a logo for the film, not within the confines of a normal advertisement but "superimposed over pages of stock quotes or weather reports" (Orwall 2001, p. B8).

Perhaps we should not be surprised. Marketers are constantly searching for previously unused spaces on which to project advertising images. Company names and logos have become commonplace on apparel, though not so long ago they were limited to labels hidden inside garments. Ads are now cropping up on the walls and columns of parking garages that, for better or worse, were previously a dull gray. Television broadcasters, perhaps taking a tip from the banner ads made popular by dot-com companies, are placing network logos and ads for upcoming programs along the margins of television screens.

However, this new idea—superimposing the ominous shadow of a flying dinosaur on the news pages of daily newspapers to give readers a subtle, almost subliminal reminder of the movie—is something quite different. As a marketer, I love it. It is creative and imaginative. Not often enough can we say that about advertising and sales promotion schemes. As an ethicist, however, I have some worries about the incorporation of advertising messages into editorial content.

There are valid reasons for this concern. At all major newspapers, magazines, and radio and television stations, there are long-standing policies of keeping the sanctity of editorial content inviolate. As a society, we trust the media to give us relatively honest and unbiased reporting of news. Whether marketers like it or not, the public does not put the same faith and trust in advertising and promotional messages. So when a newspaper runs an ad that is formatted to look like a news story, it is surrounded with a border labeling it as an advertisement. When a television station runs an "infomercial," it tells its viewing audience periodically during the broadcast that the information about the product is indeed paid for by the company that produced it. We worry when children's programs blur the difference between entertainment and advertising by using cartoon figures both as product logos and as story-line characters. We strongly criticize a newspaper or magazine that soft-pedals or actually refuses to run a story—for example, on smoking and cancer—because of pressure from its tobacco company advertisers.

And so, as intrigued and pleased as I am by the shadowy dinosaur showing up on my newspaper pages, I have three levels of concern that I label "Fuddy-duddy," "The Camel's Nose," and "What Price Morality?"

Perhaps all moralists run the risk of being seen as fuddy-duddies. Too often, they are perceived as Puritan preachers in stiff white collars who get in the way of having some good, clean fun or protest against an innocent scheme for making a bit of money. "Where is the harm?" we ask, and indeed this is an important question in any ethical discussion. Where is the harm in livening up the usually dull reports of stock quotes with the subtle image of a pteranodon? Isn't this just a lighthearted way to promote a new family movie? Isn't anyone who would object to such playfulness just being a fuddy-duddy?

I suppose so, but a more thoughtful answer leads to my second level of concern. If we allow the camel to get a nose under the tent, will the rest of the ungainly, unwanted animal soon follow? There are important principles at stake. We believe that commercial messages should not be hidden. We believe that consumers should not be tricked in any way. The apocryphal story about popcorn and sodas being advertised subliminally during movies is sure to draw protests. Because we do not have high levels of trust in advertisers and their messages—visions of snake-oil salesmen come to mind—we insist that at the very least, those messages come at us clearly labeled.

We also believe, as previously mentioned, that editorial and advertising content in newspapers and other media must be kept separate. It is not being melodramatic to say that the proper functioning of government and society relies on this. If we allow the image of a flying dinosaur to appear in the midst of stock quotes as a playful means of promoting *Jurassic Park III*, aren't we allowing the camel to get a nose under the edge of the tent? Are we safer just sticking with the principle of separating advertising from editorial content and not allowing *any* infringement on the rule?

Furthermore, just who will decide right from wrong; who will decide what is allowable and what is not? There are no laws that prohibit the blending of commercial and editorial content. There are no regulatory bodies charged with that function. To date, the important principle of separation has been maintained by the publishers and editors of newspapers and magazines and the owners and station managers of radio and television stations. They have done a remarkably good job. Self-regulation has generally worked quite well—so far.

This brings us to the third level of my concerns: What price morality? The *Journal* reports that many newspapers have refused to run the dinosaur image on their news pages, but those that ran the image argue that economic pressures pushed them to do so. Advertising revenue is in a slump for almost all media, and newspapers are scrambling to find new sources. In an era of tight budgets and a sharp focus on cost cutting, are moral principles fair game to be relaxed or ignored? We have seen major corporations give up long-held policies against layoffs when economic pressures threatened. We have seen other examples of companies that, beset with heightened competition and an increased threat to their profits, give up policies of producing in the United States and move production offshore. One of the most common excuses for violating a moral principle is that "Everybody else is doing it."

These are valid concerns that cannot be ignored. The inevitable result of this line of argument is that moral principles are followed, if at all, only in periods of prosperity. Or, only the most profitable companies can afford to abide by those principles. What kind of message is being sent to the newspaper's entire organization by a publisher who breaks or bends an important policy to gain an extra few thousand dollars in advertising revenue? Under these conditions, acting ethically and recognizing a corporation's social responsibility become penalties for doing well, a form of corporate noblesse oblige.

For all the energy and concern that management scholars expend attempting to show that corporations that behave ethically produce better financial results—so far, this is a will-o'-the-wisp area of research—others believe that moral principles imply economic sacrifice. When faced with a moral choice, we presume that there is an attractive alternative. If there weren't, it wouldn't be a choice. There is an inevitable tension at some level between economic and ethical pressures; our great challenge is to find the proper balance. Just as we cannot envision ignoring the economic necessities of corporations to make a *satisfactory* profit, we also cannot sacrifice our principles when the economic pressure mounts.

So, when we see the shadow of a flying reptile dinosaur superimposed on the news pages of our newspapers, let's acknowledge the marketing creativity behind the idea. But let's also urge media executives not to cave in so readily on a principle so important as the separation and clear identification of commercial messages. The gradual erosion of that principle may be more troubling, more ominous, and certainly more real than any pteranodon.

1. What are the policies of print and broadcast media regarding the separation of editorial content and advertising? What is the rationale?

2. If creativity is the nose of the camel, what are the characteristics of the unwanted animal that follow?

3. Do moral principles imply economic sacrifice? If so, what is the proper response from corporate leaders?

25

Creativity or Deception? Cross-Marketing and Infomercials

An increasingly complex relationship has developed between Hollywood and Madison Avenue that has led to a frenzy of product placement and cross-marketing. Product placement is the practice of using brand name items in movies or on television, sometimes in exchange for a fee paid by the manufacturer to the producer of the entertainment. If the script calls for an actor to be seen quaffing a soft drink, PepsiCo might pay thousands of dollars to make sure that the soft drink is a Pepsi and that it is clearly visible for a second or two to the viewing public. Cross-marketing is the joint promotion of consumer products and a movie. For example, McDonald's may make a deal with Disney for the exclusive rights over the next ten years to promote toys of Disney movie characters in its restaurants.

As traditional media—newspapers, magazines, television, radio, billboards, and so forth—become more saturated with advertising and as consumers become more resistant, marketing managers search for new and creative ways to promote products. A common tactic is to make ads look less like ads and slip them in front of potential customers in unexpected formats. At this point, ethical questions arise. Do consumers have the need and the right to know whether they are viewing or hearing paid advertising from the product's manufacturer? Do advertisers have some moral, not to mention legal, obligation to be certain their messages are understood to be promotional and, therefore, self-serving? Or should advertisers have free rein in getting products and promotional information in front of consumers, relying on consumers' good sense to accept or refuse them?

Some examples are more serious than others. I believe that most examples of product placement are at the benign end of the spectrum. If an actor picks up a soft drink and we can identify that it is a Pepsi or a Coke,

I see no harm done. Perhaps there will be a line in the credits that the manufacturer paid a promotional fee. Even in the absence of such a notice, I do not believe an ethical violation is taking place.

At the other end of the spectrum, true deception is unethical because the viewer may be harmed. A pharmaceutical manufacturer must not dress an actor in a doctor's gown to advertise some over-the-counter drug, because viewers might believe they are receiving medical advice rather than a promotional message. Nor would it be ethical for an advertiser to use a newspaper-column format for newspaper advertising without clearly identifying the material as an ad, because the reader might believe that the message was the opinion of the newspaper and not a profit-seeking promotion.

Infomercials are another good example of potentially harmful deception. Advertisers design these lengthy commercials to look as much like a straight news broadcast as possible, so the television station must repeatedly notify viewers that they are watching ads.

In between these two poles, there are many advertising and promotional formats that are subject to judgment. Especially problematic are those ads that target vulnerable populations, such as the elderly or children, because these groups may be less able to differentiate advertising from editorial messages. Concerns should be raised if cartoon characters are used to promote a product, especially if the product is incorporated into a cartoon story.

Blurring the distinction between advertising and editorial copy and camouflaging promotional messages may be effective ways to reach more potential customers more frequently. After all, if viewers do not know they are watching an ad, they will be less likely to switch channels or make a trip to the refrigerator.

However, there are two significant risks involved. The first is to invite some sort of government regulation, especially if the tactics are perceived as falling at the harmful end of the spectrum. The second risk is even more important: to risk losing customers' goodwill. Customers do not like to feel foolish, and they certainly do not like to be deceived. To promote products in an underhanded, albeit creative, manner will only bring a short-lived benefit if customers retaliate by patronizing competitors that advertise in more traditional, straightforward, and above-board ways.

Marketers have the responsibility of deciding at which point creativity becomes deception. I applaud marketers who, rather than use camouflage, make their ads so interesting and entertaining that the audience enjoys them. The message is received clearly, and marketing moves closer to becoming a cooperative rather than an adversarial relationship.

1. Does cross-marketing have inherent ethical problems? Does product placement? If so, what are they?

2. Is a caveat emptor (buyer beware) approach really all that is needed in contemporary times?

3. At what point in a promotion can deception overtake truthfulness?

DISTRIBUTION

Introduction

Of marketing's four P's, the least understood, at least by nonmarketers, is place, or what marketers more commonly call distribution. It is clear enough what products are. Consumers must deal with prices on a daily basis. They are barraged by several thousand promotion messages every day from the time they are able to understand what they see and hear, and therefore advertising especially is no mystery. But channels of distribution and intermediaries? These are not everyday phrases, and the functions of these intermediaries—wholesalers, brokers, agents, and some retailers—are only dimly understood by nonmarketers.

It is not surprising, then, that the moral dimensions of distribution are addressed and debated less often than issues such as product liability, fair prices, and dishonest advertising. Those problems affect consumers directly, which is another reason they are addressed more often. They have more widespread appeal, and they receive more attention from advocacy groups and the media. Distribution issues, in contrast, frequently begin with struggles between two or more businesses, rather than consumers and businesses. Nevertheless, important and interesting issues do arise from this segment of marketing.

Even in the simplest and most common distribution channel, which consists of a manufacturer, a retailer, and a consumer, many problems can arise at different levels. There are problems that involve two parties on the same level—for example, one manufacturer versus another or one retailer pitted against another. There are also problems between the levels of distribution—vertical problems, if you will—in which the manufacturer's interests clash with the interests of the retailer or the consumer.

Many of these issues have to do with power. Which firm is bigger and stronger, and how does it use this power to its advantage? Consider Procter & Gamble, General Electric, or Microsoft. How do these billion-dollar corporations treat the much smaller retailers and wholesalers that distribute their products?

A small women's apparel retailer, for example, has difficulty competing with Macy's and Nordstrom for fair treatment from large manufacturers such as Liz Claiborne or Levi Strauss. By law, manufacturers must offer their products at the same price to both large and small retailers, unless they can prove that there are real and significant cost savings in dealing with the large retailer. Such proof can be difficult for manufacturers to produce. The result is that small retailers can often buy the same style for the same price from Liz Claiborne as Macy's can.

There are less obvious ways, however, for the manufacturer to favor its larger customers. It can ship its new seasonal styles to Macy's first and to the smaller retailer last, which causes the smaller merchant to have a shorter selling period than Macy's. Or perhaps, being last on the priority list, the small merchant *never* receives the merchandise because the manufacturer may exhaust its inventory of the style before shipping to smaller customers. If the style sells well, Macy's will have a chance to reorder it, perhaps before the small retailer even receives its first shipment, or the manufacturer may use the inventory allotted to small retailers to fill reorders for Macy's and Nordstrom. If the style sells poorly, the large stores may still have an advantage. Macy's will find a reason to return slow-selling items to Liz Claiborne, a reason Liz Claiborne would never accept from a small retailer. Nordstrom may use its clout to demand "markdown money" from the manufacturer, whereas the small store might never think of this and would probably be refused even if it did.

Under other circumstances, the position of power may be reversed: It may reside with the retailer. As Wal-Mart grew quickly and dramatically to become the largest retailer in the world, these problems have become more apparent. The manufacturers that produce private-label merchandise for Wal-Mart, Target, or JCPenney may become overly dependent on one of those retailers. In some cases, the retailer may be the manufacturer's only customer. When the buyer for a giant chain store asks for a better price for a special promotion or asks the manufacturer to absorb some of the chain's inventory expense, does the small manufacturer dare refuse this request from its only customer? Under such circumstances, there is certainly a moral dimension in the business dealings between the two firms because one is so much larger and more powerful than the other. JCPenney, Wal-Mart, Target, and every other giant retailer must consider how far to push their suppliers. There are strictly business-related considerations, of course. Push too far, and Target could lose a valued supplier. Push too little, and the chain may lose a competitive advantage because its competitors receive better prices on similar items from their suppliers. There are ethical questions as well. Is it fair for Target to squeeze too hard if a small manufacturer has agreed, perhaps under duress, to devote all of its production to satisfying its most important, or perhaps only, customer? If this dependency relationship exists, whether by the design of the chain store or not, does the chain have an obligation not to take a precipitous action that would jeopardize the very existence of the manufacturer?

The ethical problems with "horizontal" distribution have received more publicity and discussion. Again, Wal-Mart, because of its dominant size, has been the focal point of late. Some communities, notably in the New England states, have protested and sometimes even blocked the arrival of a Wal-Mart store because of the threat Wal-Mart poses to the long-established local merchants. The local stores argue that they will never be able to compete against the giant retailer and that Wal-Mart's low prices and huge assortments will force them out of business. They also argue that the traditional downtown shopping areas in their cities will be threatened with extinction and that the "character" of the community will be changed forever if Wal-Mart moves in. There are case histories to bolster these arguments.

Members of the community—that is, potential customers—have taken both sides on this issue. Sometimes they side with the local merchants and are willing to give up the low prices proffered by a nearby Wal-Mart in favor of the familiarity and charm of smaller, more neighborly stores. At other times and in other places—perhaps where there is little or no charm to salvage—a town's citizens have welcomed a giant discount store. *The Washington Post* featured an unflattering story about Battle Mountain, Nev., that claimed that many of the town's citizens listed a Wal-Mart store as the "improvement" they wanted most (see Weingarten 2001).

There are other issues that have a moral dimension as well. Does a retailer that has been supported by a community for several decades have an obligation to stay in the community even after it has deteriorated and the location is no longer profitable? Some argue that because the community made an "investment" in the retailer and became a stakeholder, the retailer "owes" the community some degree of loyalty in return.

What are the retailer's responsibilities for some of these ethical dilemmas as they apply to manufacturers? Should a retailer share the manufacturer's liability for harm done by products that are unsafe in design or in production? Does the retailer have any obligation to test potentially dangerous products before selling them? Does the store become an agent of the manufacturer in some moral, if not legal, sense?

If a manufacturer uses contractors, either at home or abroad, that manufacture goods under unfair working conditions or use child or slave labor, does the retailer share in the responsibility by stocking and selling those goods? Wal-Mart became embroiled in this very issue by selling Kathie Lee Gifford label merchandise. The manufacturer has been accused of using child labor to make the garments.

Over the past two decades, an enormous amount of criticism has been directed at cigarette manufacturers for making a product that causes so much damage to human health and marketing that product without owning up to its addictive and often lethal properties. Almost no attention has been focused, however, on the responsibilities of the retailers from whom consumers buy cigarettes. No one doubts that retailers are aware of the medical effects associated with smoking. Yet retailers willingly buy cigarettes and sell them to the public. Should retailers be held responsible and share in the liability associated with smoking and its public health consequences?

In the essays that follow, a few of these issues are discussed, but much more work should be done to uncover and analyze the moral problems of the distribution side of marketing.

26

Is There Such a Thing as "Ethical Competition"?

In Santa Cruz, Calif., a few years ago, a new "superstore" branch of a national bookstore chain opened for business directly across the city's main shopping street from Bookstore Santa Cruz, one of the largest and best-known bookstores on the West Coast. Not only is Bookstore Santa Cruz something of an institution in that city, but its owner, Neal Coonerty, was one of Santa Cruz's most active civic leaders. Coonerty was facing a much larger competitor that would use its size and buying power to offer books at rock-bottom prices. If these circumstances sound familiar, perhaps it is due to the popular movie, *You've Got Mail*, which used this problem as the unlikely setting for a romance.

Small stores facing much larger competitors is hardly an isolated problem. Family-owned general merchandise and hardware stores fear being run out of business wherever Wal-Mart opens a new store. The arrival of a new Blockbuster portends hard times for local video stores. Thirty years ago, local merchants on the Monterey Peninsula of California feared the opening of a new Macy's in their community. And so it goes with the opening of any new branch of a dominant chain store, or category killer: Home Depot, PETsMART, Toys "R" Us, and the like.

Common wisdom among marketers is that the local merchants must find some competitive advantage of their own. If they cannot compete on price and assortment, they must carve out a niche that the giants cannot fill that will give them the upper hand, such as personal service, better knowledge of customers, or a specialty left untouched by the chain store. This is a familiar subject for marketing strategy, but what about marketing ethics?

The Santa Cruz bookstore version of the David and Goliath story set me thinking about the nature of competition. Does competition necessarily mean ultimate victory for one and crushing defeat for another, or is there a more civilized level of competition?

I was born and raised in a midwestern city where two local, family-owned department stores competed vigorously for many decades. Both stores were prosperous, and the two families remained friendly throughout. Even the classic retail competition between Macy's and Gimbel's in New York City, as aggressive as it was, was not a battle to the death. Both stores realized that their ongoing competition was essential to the economic health of Herald Square as a shopping area.

Yet we compete to win. If there is a winner, then there must be a loser. Can there be and should there be limits on how vigorously businesses compete? At what point should a competitor back off and allow the opponent a chance to recoup? This problem is made more difficult by absentee ownership. Whereas two families in a midwestern city may be able to arrive at some mutually acceptable level of competition, it is unlikely that two chain store managers, pressured for improved economic performance by their respective corporate headquarters that are far removed from the site of the battle, would decide to "go easy" on each other and pass up an opportunity to grab market share.

As efficient as a free market is, it does not help resolve this kind of question. One of the dilemmas of capitalism is that though competition is an absolute necessity, the natural workings of a competitive system push markets to ever greater concentration. Weaker firms are pushed out of the contest, only the fittest survive, and the number of competitors diminishes.

"Ethical competition" may be difficult to define, much less to achieve, but it is not an oxymoron. There are two yardsticks by which it can be measured. The first yardstick measures the structure of the industry. A strategy whereby a firm eliminates competition to exploit monopolistic power is unethical (not to mention illegal). It fails the ethical test on utilitarian grounds, because the net cost to society—the loss of small businesses and, therefore, the reduction of competition—is greater than the net benefit. Wal-Mart and Microsoft have been accused of resorting to this level of competition.

The second yardstick, which I call "excessive zeal," is by far the more difficult to apply. Excessive zeal applies to a competitor that captures too much market share. Analogies from football might be "piling on" or "running up the score." An executive of the previously discussed bookstore chain allegedly warned Neal Coonerty that he would "crush" Bookstore Santa Cruz. If the warning was more than mere bluster and if it became part of the chain's business strategy, it goes beyond the limit of ethical competition.

Again, I plead for business managers to practice restraint because it is unlikely and impractical to expect formal legislation to dictate the proper degree of competition. I believe there is a viable level of competition that does not entail annihilating the opponent. It will probably require optimizing, rather than maximizing, profits. As difficult as ethical competition may be to define precisely, it will allow the lion to lie down with the lamb. The category-killer bookstore will coexist with Bookstore Santa Cruz; Wal-Mart will compete with local merchants in the same community. This is more than just good ethics, it is good business as well. It reduces the need for more onerous government regulation, and it preserves marketplace diversity from which both buyers and sellers can benefit.

1. Does a capitalist system intrinsically favor a monopoly that forces weak firms out of the market? If so, is there anything unethical about this, or is it simply a fact of life?

2. If a firm adopts "ethical competition" and avoids forcing its competitors out of business, is it ignoring its responsibilities to shareholders?

27

Retailers' Obligations to Depressed Areas

It happens all the time. The income level of a shopping area begins to slide; retail stores leave for greener pastures as their leases expire; the neighborhood is left with rent-to-own stores, adult bookstores, or empty spaces; and the cycle takes a turn for the worse.

What obligations do stores have to the communities that have supported them for 10, 20, or 30 years? Given the constraints of lease conditions, all businesses, including retailers, must be free to choose the most suitable and profitable location, rent, and ambience for their operations. Local governments impose zoning restrictions, but with that exception, location decisions should be based on economic considerations and the marketplace exchanges between lessors and lessees. To do otherwise—to insist that a firm operate in an area not of its own choosing or prevent it from moving to a more profitable site—would place a costly burden on the firm. Eventually, the results would be higher prices and less efficient operations.

So far, so good. Still to be faced, however, are the problems of a neighborhood that is struggling to arrest its decline but is left without adequate retail stores to serve it. Residents who are the least able to afford the additional cost and inconvenience are forced to travel further to shop. Is this strictly society's or government's concern, or do businesses bear some obligation? Certainly there is a moral dimension to this problem and to businesses' decision to relocate. Is it immoral for a business to move to a more upscale and more profitable location if doing so leaves its current customers without comparable services?

Utilitarianism is one framework for analyzing this problem. The positive result—the firm's improved profitability—is relatively easy to quantify. The negative results for the neighborhood, especially the inconvenience suffered by the residents, are difficult to measure. Therefore, a strictly utilitarian analysis is inconclusive.

Another possible framework is to compare the parties' rights. In this free-enterprise economy, businesses have a right to choose their locations on the basis of economic criteria and are limited only by zoning restrictions. Residents of a neighborhood are not accorded the right to convenient shopping, so it is reasonable to conclude that it is not unethical for the business to move.

Justice, however, makes the pendulum swing at least part way toward the rights of neighborhood residents. In this framework, benefits and burdens should be shared by all, and according to philosopher John Rawls, decisions must be made to improve the relative standing of the least advantaged in society. It simply is not fair if inhabitants of a low-income neighborhood are deprived of essential services.

To carry the analysis further, it is important to recognize the differences among the almost infinite number of businesses. One difference is size. The owner and operator of a single store could hardly be considered unethical were he or she to move the business to a more promising neighborhood if staying might result in the demise of the business. Conversely, for Sears, JCPenney, or Safeway, keeping a store in a depressed location would not threaten the vitality of the corporation.

Another difference is the type of business. Some retailers are more important to a community than others. A neighborhood might suffer some inconvenience without an appliance store or a toy store, but it would get along reasonably well. The loss of a food retailer, however, would inflict much more harm on the community, especially if it is the only one in the area. In other words, we must evaluate to what degree the businesses and their services are essential.

Yet another difference among businesses is profitability. In an ethical analysis, it matters if the business is actually losing money in its current location. The amount of losses is also important. In 1992, after the riots and devastation in South Central Los Angeles, Ralphs and Vons, two of the region's major supermarket chains, reopened their damaged stores despite the economic advantages of moving to safer and more profitable locations. These firms showed great corporate social responsibility.

Would it have been unethical if Ralphs and Vons abandoned their damaged stores? Given the foregoing criteria, the answer is yes. Both supermarket chains are profitable, multibillion dollar businesses. Reopening their stores in the blighted area was not a threat to the viability of either firm, and both firms were providing essential services to the neighborhood.

Customers are principal stakeholders for any firm. Another stakeholder, though the relationship is less direct and clear, is the community in which the firm does business. Sorting out the nature and strength of these relationships—in other words, analyzing a firm's obligations and responsibilities to a community—is never a simple, straightforward matter. Exceptions to many accepted rules may be necessary.

The social problems that deteriorating neighborhoods create are very real and must be addressed. Two things are certain. First, it is not only the government that should bear the responsibility for these problems. The business community, especially the retailers that can contribute either to the problem or to its solution, must be involved. Second, the economics of the problem cannot be ignored, but neither can the moral dilemma.

1. Which stakeholders should a business take into consideration when deciding whether to move from a depressed area?

2. What frameworks of ethical analysis should be used to make a decision of this kind?

3. How do the nature and circumstances of the business affect the decision-making process?

Stocklifting: An Ethical Analysis

The term "stocklifting" describes a marketing tactic in which a manufacturer buys all of a rival's product from a retailer and replaces it with its own product to gain access to the retailer's shelves. The rival's product is then sold to a liquidator at a steep discount, and it eventually goes to an off-price retailer or out of the United States for sale overseas.

According to Yumiko Ono (1998) of *The Wall Street Journal*, stocklifting has become increasingly commonplace, and it involves merchandise across a wide spectrum of categories—from gloves to glue. It is a costly tactic for a manufacturer, because the discount needed to attract a liquidator is enormous. However, it may be worth the cost because the manufacturer gains instant market share and the opportunity to establish an ongoing relationship with the retailer.

Frankly, my gut reaction to this tactic is negative. It doesn't smell right to me. Setting aside legal questions—Is stocklifting an anti-competitive practice?—I want to consider the ethical issues. Let's perform a modest ethical analysis starting with the question, "Who is being hurt and who is being helped by this practice?" This seems to be a straightforward approach.

My first step is to consider the customer. To keep things simple, assume that the prices and qualities of the two rival products are similar. The customer appears to be no better or worse off as a result of the switch. Arguably, it is better for the customer if the retailer offers both products so that the customer has a choice. But both before and after the stocklifting, the customer is presented with only one product line, so stocklifting itself does not put the customer in a worse position.

Or does it? Marketing costs, in theory, are supposed to add value to the product for the customer. If this stocklifting tactic costs the manufacturer, say, $300,000, what added value is there for the customer? Presumably, the customer pays a higher price to cover this marketing expense and does not benefit, so the customer is worse off as a result of the switch.

But that is not the final word. Customer A may be worse off, but Customer B will buy the gloves or the glue from an off-price retailer at half or more off the normal retail price. Customer B has surely benefited. In this position, costs and benefits must be balanced for customers as a group.

What about the other parties involved in the transaction? The first manufacturer, whose goods were bought and replaced, seems no worse off as a result of stocklifting. It has already profited from the initial sale to the retailer. It is true that the manufacturer no longer has the opportunity for continued business with the retailer, but that was never guaranteed in the first place. In theory, the retailer might have decided to switch suppliers after the first shipment. This manufacturer could also, in theory, pull the same tactic on its competitor with some other retailer, which would increase the cost of doing business for all the manufacturers in this industry. The second manufacturer, the stocklifter, and the retailer are presumably better off as a result of stocklifting, or they would not have entered into an agreement.

What, then, is the reason for my concern and negative reaction? What gives this tactic a bad smell? Ethicists would tell me that there is another, quite different approach for looking at ethical problems. This framework for analysis is called "deontology," and it involves rights, values, principles, and justice. This is where I turn for further analysis.

Surely, the abuse of power is unjust and a violation of rights. The second manufacturer, perhaps under pressure from the retailer, was willing and able to spend $300,000 to muscle the rival's product off the shelves. As a result, the first producer is denied the opportunity to sell merchandise to the retailer's customers and to establish some degree of brand preference or brand loyalty with that market segment. This means that, as with the practice of slotting fees, in which a large retailer requires a manufacturer to pay for one or more "facings" on the retailer's shelves, the larger and financially stronger manufacturers have a competitive advantage.

Size, financial resources, and even the willingness to gamble can give any firm an advantage over another in the competitive marketplace. For this reason, small, locally owned merchants have always dreaded the arrival of a big discount or department store. Doesn't the larger firm always have an advantage over a smaller competitor? Is this advantage unfair?

The answers to these questions are "yes" and "not necessarily." Smaller competitors know about these risks when they enter the marketplace. Still, stocklifting seems underhanded. There is collusion between the manufacturer and the retailer to eliminate another manufacturer's goods from the stores, and the switch is performed overnight (often literally) with no opportunity for the competitor to respond. It also means that the retailer is not performing the task that justifies its role in the distribution chain: offering the most attractive assortment of products to its customers. Instead, the assortment of items and brands is simply based on which manufacturer is willing to spend enough money to stocklift.

Most of the marketing ethics literature focuses on manufacturers and their relationships and responsibilities to their customers. Stocklifting illustrates how retailers use their size and power to exact concessions from manufacturers, sometimes to the detriment of consumers. The power of certain retailers has been made more apparent in recent years by the phenomenal growth of Wal-Mart and the consolidation of firms in many retail sectors.

With greater power comes greater responsibility. Pressuring manufacturers to stocklift and pay slotting fees to gain access to a retailer's shelves is an abuse of power. Sometimes ethical analyses—balancing costs and benefits, protecting rights, seeking justice—do not clearly determine if an activity is right or wrong. Sometimes a marketer must go with how the activity smells.

1. Is stocklifting just one more size-related problem that a small manufacturer must face in the competitive marketplace, or is it really an unfair practice?

2. Should the government step into this situation with legislation and regulation—perhaps based on anti-trust laws—to eliminate stocklifting, or should retailers and manufacturers be left to police themselves?

PRIVACY

Introduction

Privacy is a familiar issue in business ethics literature. Most of the attention over the years has focused on employees' rights to privacy and how to define those rights. Do employers have the right to search an employee's desk, locker, or personal belongings? Can an employer monitor an employee's telephone calls, e-mail messages, or Internet browsing without the employee's knowledge and consent? Can an employer insist on a drug test as a condition for employment? These questions are commonly found in any standard textbook's treatment of the subject.

In recent years, more and more attention has focused on the privacy rights of an organization's customers, and thus the marketing function of the organization becomes the center of concern. This is not an entirely new development. It comes as no surprise that companies have used information about consumers for their own purposes. A purchase of a men's shirt at Nordstrom may result in the customer receiving a Nordstrom men's sales catalog a month or two later, whether it was requested or not. A purchase from L.L.Bean may result in the customer receiving several of that mail order firm's specialty catalogs.

The privacy issue becomes more problematic if firms profit from the information they have collected by selling it to others. For decades, consumers have been aware that subscription lists of magazines and other publications could be bought and sold. A subscriber to *The Atlantic Monthly* might expect to receive occasional solicitations from publishers of other literary magazines. In addition, various charities sell their lists of contributors. A donor to the American Cancer Society is likely to receive letters of solicitation from other nonprofit health organizations.

There has been little concern over these uses of personal information because the potential for harm is limited. Direct marketers offer the rationale that they provide consumers with useful information about new products: how they work, how much they cost, and where to purchase them. At worst, the daily dose of "junk" mail grows beyond what consumers (or postal carriers) might wish, or consumers receive too many annoying telemarketing calls just as they are about to sit down to dinner. These are valid nuisances, but they do not pose serious ethical problems.

The proliferation of credit cards and their widespread use have created another set of potential problems for marketers. Visa, MasterCard, and American Express have an extraordinary amount of information about consumers' buying patterns that marketers of all kinds would love to have. So far, the credit card companies have resisted the temptation to profit from the sale of this information to others.

However, two forces have recently moved the infringement on consumer privacy, which was previously a relatively minor nuisance, into the limelight of serious social and ethical concern. The first is the meteoric growth of the Internet as an electronic marketplace, and the second is the rapid development of technology that manages and manipulates vast quantities of information about customers. As with so many moral matters, this has created a dilemma. Although consumers may welcome the ability of large organizations to recognize them as individuals, they may worry that those organizations will be tempted to profit from information about consumers' lives and buying habits by selling that information.

I have been a customer of Amazon.com for several years. I confess that I get a little twinge of satisfaction when I log on to Amazon's Web site and see my name immediately appear on the screen. It is a little bit like the joy of walking into a store and having the owner, or even a salesperson, call me by name, which happens too infrequently these days. Amazon no longer needs to ask for my address; it knows it and makes it available each time I make a purchase. It even remembers the addresses of all the people to whom I have sent books, and it keeps that information ready for me if I should need it.

Amazon's personal service goes much further. It remembers what books I have purchased, and each time I log on, Amazon recommends books on related subjects that might interest me. Retail organizations have only dreamed that their salespeople could offer such service. There are no moral issues in this example yet, only wonderful customer benefits.

If I buy a book about sailing from Amazon, that information is valuable to Amazon, but it is also valuable to others. The publisher of *Sailing* magazine, for example, would love to know the names and e-mail and physical mailing addresses of people who are interested in the sport. Amazon could easily profit by selling my readily available personal information to the publisher. Is this unethical, especially if it is done without my knowledge or consent? How much harm is done, after all? At the very worst, I may receive several solicitations to subscribe to *Sailing*. But what if I purchase a book from Amazon about the treatment of diabetes?

There are organizations that would like to receive that information as well. Pharmaceutical firms would like to know about my purchase and add me to their databases of potential customers. Of more concern, a health insurance company would also like to know about my purchase because it might use that information as a screen for granting or denying insurance coverage. Whether I am a diabetic or am just interested in reading about the subject, I might well be declined coverage if Amazon sells that information to the insurance company. Now some real harm may result from Amazon's sale of the data—more harm than simply intruding on my abstract "right" to privacy. Now it is a genuine moral issue.

A utilitarian—searching for the greatest net benefit to society—would need to weigh Amazon's financial benefit from selling the data, and perhaps the insurance company's financial benefit from avoiding a risky client, against the harm done to me from losing my privacy and medical insurance coverage. A Kantian—attempting to balance the rights of the involved parties—would need to weigh Amazon's right to use my personal information, which is its property, against my implied right to have that information kept private between Amazon and me. If Amazon sells my information to the insurance company, it uses me and my privacy as a means to the end of creating wealth for itself, rather than following Kant, who wrote that people must never be treated as "means," only as "ends" in themselves.

Who decides what information should be shared and sold in cyberspace? A computer? The person who wrote the program? A marketing manager? A finance officer searching for a new stream of revenue? Or would it serve the search for the moral high ground for customers to be allowed to decide how their personal information is used? Marketers are likely either to cede this decision to customers willingly or to be forced to do so by government regulation or by social pressures from consumer advocacy groups, the media, and so forth.

That still leaves another important question to be answered. In what form will the customer's wishes be recognized? Given the economic value of the information they possess, marketers are tempted to assume that personal information can be sold unless the customer gives specific instructions not to do so. This is the so-called opt-out provision. It is of limited value, however, for customer protection. In addition to those customers who do not much care either way, a large percentage of customers do not understand their responsibility to opt out, do not know how to act on it, or simply will never get around to opting out. The alternative solution is an opt-in provision: Marketers can use, share, or sell customer's personal information only if customers agree in advance to such an arrangement. There is no question that such a provision is less profitable for an online marketing organization, because only a small percentage of customers would agree to such an arrangement without receiving significant compensation. Yet to reach that moral high ground, the opt-in provision is necessary to ensure customers' rights to privacy.

So there we have it once again: economics versus ethics, the drive to maximize earnings to satisfy shareholders' bumping up against the responsibilities to customers. The following essays explore these concerns in more detail.

Is Privacy Dead?

Is privacy really dead, as Christine Varney (2000) suggests in a lead article in *Newsweek* magazine? Given the spate of headlines in both the business and the popular press, one might be inclined to believe that we have already witnessed the end of personal privacy. Big Business has taken over the role played by the government, Big Brother, in the novel *1984*, and it is indeed snooping on people's activities through television sets, e-mail, mobile telephones, and the Internet. Forrester Research reports that 91% of respondents to a recent poll are either extremely concerned or somewhat concerned about providing their personal data online.

The methods multinational businesses either use or will use in the near future to monitor private activities have been reported often enough, but they paint a frightening picture nonetheless. "Cookies," which are files that businesses implant in desktop computers to track consumers' travels on the Internet from one site to another, report how long consumers linger on any one site and what they look at or buy there. Information about where consumers live, what they buy, their financial situation, and their medical problems is routinely bought, sold, traded, and moved from one corporation to another, often without consumers' knowledge or permission. Unwanted ads show up at inopportune moments on personal pagers, and the long-awaited next generation of mobile telephones may ring with a sales pitch from a local business just as the phone user is driving or walking by.

Could there be a better subject for a discussion of marketing ethics? The debate over privacy has all the necessary ingredients: the ever-present struggle between ethics and economics, short-term profit versus long-term reputation and goodwill, consumers' rights to privacy versus companies' rights to free speech in advertising, the delicate balance of a corporation's responsibility to its customers and to its shareholders.

As with any truly interesting issue involving morality in marketing, there are no easy answers. There are always two or more sides to be considered. Let us explore just some of the complexities surrounding consumer privacy.

It will come as no surprise, least of all to those involved in one way or another with marketing, that to market products effectively and efficiently, marketers need to know as much as possible about how their customers behave. Consumer behavior, after all, is a major specialty within the broad field of marketing. In the United States alone, marketers spend billions of dollars each year to learn more about how, when, why, and what customers buy. Marketers have developed all kinds of methodologies for conducting this research, from straightforward surveys and focus groups to sophisticated mechanical and electronic devices for tracking customers' paths through a supermarket or across the Internet. But there is a qualitative difference in learning about what consumers *in general* do or want and what *specific* customers do or want. It may be of little concern to a customer that marketing managers know, to the second or third decimal point, how many Web sites a *typical* surfer will log on to in a normal session, but that customer may be greatly troubled to learn that marketing managers know how many and what Web sites he or she visited in a given day.

There are still other considerations. I want United Airlines to know precisely how many trips I have taken, how many miles I have flown, and to what destinations I have gone so that it will reward me in due course with free trips. There are thousands of households that allow ACNielsen to monitor their television viewing habits in exchange for a modest compensation. Procter & Gamble has sent camera crews to the homes of hundreds of its customers, with their permission, to film all (well, not quite all) of the family's activities. P&G wants to know, without relying on sometimes faulty memories, just how many times a teenage son reaches for the Jif peanut butter or how Dad squeezes the last of the toothpaste out of the tube of Crest. Nordstrom built its sterling reputation for top-notch customer service on, among other things, its salespeople who maintain records of their customers' purchases and use that information to notify them of new styles or impending promotions. In each of these examples, customers willingly sacrifice their privacy, and so we cannot say that *all* inquiries and intrusions by marketers into consumers' buying habits are bad.

There is an obvious explanation for these examples. In those situations, consumers believe that allowing companies to learn more about their activities—in effect, sacrificing some element of privacy—is more than offset by the benefit derived: better service, merchandise awards, and cash payments. This suggests, however, that privacy is not sacrosanct. Everyone is willing to bargain away some degree of privacy depending on what is received in exchange. That makes privacy seem like any other commodity.

Privacy differs, however, because consumers often claim the "right" to privacy, though they seldom inquire as to the source of this right. Is it akin to "life, liberty, and the pursuit of happiness"? Is it a natural right, or is it a right granted by law and, therefore, subject to being rescinded by a democratic process? Are the poor entitled to the same right to privacy as the wealthy? Is it a right that varies from one culture to another? Does it vary from one time to another? The last question is especially important as new technologies continuously enable marketers to invade people's privacy with greater ease and with less awareness on their part. Do complex societies and community living require the sacrifice of some rights to privacy just as some property rights are ceded for the good of the community?

The excuses that businesses offer for invading consumers' privacy are hardly convincing. When a credit card company explains that it may from time to time share customers' personal information—addresses and telephone numbers, for starters—with other companies so that customers can learn about new products and services, how many customers take this at face value? Or are customers more inclined to believe, if they think about it at all, that it is a very profitable business for the credit card company to *sell* that information over and over again in the active marketplace for demographic data?

For example, my credit card issuer recently sent me a seven-page document titled "Important Privacy Notice," which included the following as part of the bank's privacy policy: "Responsible use of information is beneficial. Information is important for meeting your needs and providing consistent service quality. Information is also the source of new ideas. The more we understand about you and your needs, the better we can suggest products and services, create new opportunities for you, and help you manage your financial assets." Who would disagree with this? But it doesn't take a cynic to think that, just maybe, the bank is really more concerned with its own profit-making opportunities than with my needs for new products or services.

There is much that we do *not* know about this aspect of consumer privacy. Moreover, acceptable ethical standards are dramatically more difficult to achieve because of rapidly evolving technology that enables businesses to gather, use, and profit from data in innovative and usually secretive ways.

This we *do* know: Businesses have at least two obligations. First, they must inform their customers about what they will and will not do with the data they collect. Second, they must offer, as well as facilitate, the opportunity for customers to choose whether their personal information can be shared with other companies. There are all sorts of details that are important as well: How "fine" is the fine print, how often is the customer reminded of the company's policies, does the company actually abide by its own stated policies, and so on. This issue is evolving on a weekly, if not a daily, basis. There is certainly a gap between business performance and public expectations. How that gap is filled will be fascinating to watch. Will it require government to regulate all businesses, or will the business community do a good enough job of self-regulating to satisfy and ease the worries of consumers?

Behind the issue of consumer privacy is the problematic buyer–seller relationship. If it is a fundamentally cooperative relationship, businesses will use personal information only in the best interests of their customers. If the relationship is fundamentally adversarial, however, businesses will continue to manage personal information as an asset so that it produces the maximum profit.

1. What are the ingredients in the struggle between ethics and economics?

2. Are there both good and bad uses for the personal information businesses collect? Give examples.

3. What are the moral responsibilities of businesses to their customers regarding the personal information businesses collect?

30

Of Chickens and Foxes: Business as the Protector of Privacy Rights

In a land far, far away lived a benevolent farmer who owned a group of chickens. Every so often, the farmer enlisted the help of a fox to guard the henhouse, but this always turned out to be a very bad idea. Time and again, the fox succumbed to his baser instincts and gobbled up a hen or two while performing his assigned task. One day, the farmer pondered this problem. He could not spend all his time watching over the chickens, and the fox really did a good job of keeping the other predators away. So the farmer made a deal with the fox. If the fox would give up eating an occasional chicken, the farmer would give him plenty of food from his own table scraps. The fox licked his chops and readily agreed to the bargain.

As the ethical and legal questions associated with privacy in e-commerce evolve, I am reminded of a fable about foxes and chickens. Scarcely a week goes by without a news release describing a technological development that will enable sellers to learn even more about the buying patterns of consumers and how consumers use products and services. For example, automobile rental companies can now install electronic devices on their cars that transmit data that show where their cars are being driven and even how fast they are going. Hertz and Avis argue that these devices aid in the recovery of stolen cars; customers are not so sure they want their activities monitored, especially without their knowledge.

Wireless telephones will soon know exactly where we are—or, more precisely, where they are. This has some clear advantages, especially for the transmission of 911 calls. Imagine standing on a street corner of an unfamiliar city with an overwhelming desire for Chinese cuisine. Merely dial up a restaurant-finder service and discover that the egg rolls and mu shu pork you crave are just two blocks down the street. There is a dark side as well. This same technology in telephones can transmit to marketers exactly where we have traveled to add more data to their information storehouses on our shopping and buying patterns. The telephone can also be programmed to call us as we pass a retailer promoting a year-end clearance sale.

As intriguing and attractive as these new technological wonders may be, they pose a dilemma for society: Consumers must give up not only hard-earned money to buy them but also some privacy. Consumers are attracted by the benefits, but they are worried about being protected from the exploitation of sellers through the invasion of their privacy. Almost everyone agrees that there are such things as rights to privacy, even if it is uncertain where these rights originate or how far they extend. It is also uncertain who should be the protector and guarantor of these rights. Will there be new laws and regulations? Will there be a new government agency for such matters? Will consumer advocacy groups rise to the challenge and acquire enough authority to fill the role? Or should society rely on the workings of the market?

As unlikely as the last alternative sounds, and as little historical precedent there may be for relying on the vicissitudes of the market for consumer protection, at least two developments point toward it. The March, 2001, issue of *The Atlantic Monthly* featured as its cover story a lengthy article by Toby Lester on "The Reinvention of Privacy." This article was unique not for its catalog of privacy problems but for the possible answer: The growing need for privacy protection is creating a business opportunity in its own right.

The first development comes from Zero-Knowledge Systems of Montreal, Canada, an entrepreneurial company that has seized on this business opportunity and now offers something it calls "anonymizer technology." For less than $50, a consumer can buy the premium service that absolutely guarantees online privacy, according to the company. "By wrapping information in multiple layers of the strongest encryption available ... Zero-Knowledge allows customers to establish as many as five untraceable pseudonymous digital identities, or 'nyms,' with which to browse the Web and send e-mail." The thrust of the article? The market for privacy protection will be so strong that it will generate more of these new products and make it profitable for more new companies to manufacture and sell them. The workings of the market, which have given rise to the problem, will spawn a solution; the foxes will in fact guard the hens.

Not all of these new products will originate in some entrepreneur's garage. The second development comes from Microsoft, which wants to make computers smart enough to protect privacy against invasion, just to the degree that each user chooses. The technology will be built into Microsoft's new Internet Explorer 6 browser, and it is based on the Platform for Privacy Preferences, or P3P, which will enable each user to enjoy the wonders of cyberspace with a chosen degree of privacy.

Choose a medium level of privacy protection, and you get the following: "Blocks third-party cookies that do not have a compact privacy policy ... [or] that use personally identifiable information without your implicit consent." Change the setting to high protection, and the software blocks cookies from anyone who does not have a P3P policy. Microsoft is hoping and betting that the clamor for protection will become so great that e-commerce firms—from start-ups to giants such as Amazon and eBay—will be forced to adopt the P3P protocols and policies. In turn, Microsoft Internet Explorer 6 will become all the more indispensable and the browser of choice.

These are exciting possibilities: new-age solutions to new-age problems. The potential stumbling blocks, however, are anything but new. The history of the relationship of business, consumers, and the government leads consumers to be wary of relying solely on business to protect them. Invariably, consumers have had to turn to the government to guarantee an adequate level of protection.

The hens were of mixed minds about this deal between the fox and the farmer. Some were pleased because they thought the fox had often been maligned and that his reputation could not be as bad as others thought. Others were grateful that some other unknown protector was not going to take over the job. Still others wanted the farmer to watch over them and had lingering doubts about trusting the fox.

1. Will the workings of the market suffice to deal with the problems of online privacy? Why, or why not?

2. Under what circumstances can and should society rely on the business community for solutions to the ethical problems it creates?

31

Life as a Series of Trade-Offs

What busy lives we lead! From month to month, year to year, we seem to have an increasing number of tasks, responsibilities, opportunities, and challenges filling up every spare minute. Ask any parent of preteen or teenage children about needing to arrange rides to practices, games, appointments, playdates, sleepovers, and the like. When both parents in a household are working, the situation is much more chaotic. Who wouldn't welcome some help remembering and organizing all the things they need to do? Neil Irwin (2001) in *The Washington Post* reported on a company, LifeMinders Inc., that is offering just such a service.

I visited the LifeMinders Web site and learned that the company will remind me in advance of my best friend's birthday, advise me to change the oil in my car, and give me tips on potty training my two-year-old (if I had one). What a wonderful service! All I need to do is send the company quite a bit of information about myself: the usual demographic data such as e-mail address, who my best friends are and when they were born, what kind of car I drive, and the ages of my children. There are many other ways LifeMinders will help me organize my life, all of which require even more information. At this point, I was confronted with the first of many trade-offs: Should I sacrifice privacy concerns for the convenience of these services?

LifeMinders offers information about its privacy policies near the bottom of its Web site (www.lifeminders.com/lifeminder30/imsite/utilities/privacy.asp). My guess is that not many visitors would bother searching for this, but given my research interests, I did. Every other visitor should as well. The company advises the following:

◆It would collect only the information needed to provide its services. I could withhold some of the information, but this would limit the level of service the company could provide.

◆It would share my personal information with its "marketing partners," so I could receive special offers by e-mail or telephone.

138

◆It employs outside companies and people as "agents" that will help analyze my personal information, so these agents would need to have access to my personal information.

◆It will place a "cookie" in my computer; I can set my browser to reject the cookie, but this may result in sections of the company's Web site not operating properly for me.

◆It "may include certain links in [its] e-mails that will allow [it] to monitor whether [I] access specific content or advertisements" contained in that e-mail.

◆It will take "reasonable precautions" to protect my personal information, but I should "not expect that such information will be absolutely free from intrusion."

◆It will send me e-mail messages with links to other sites, but LifeMinders is not responsible for the privacy policies or content of these third parties.

◆It will share my personal information with other parties pursuant to a sale or merger of the company. (Indeed, LifeMinders was recently acquired by Cross Media Marketing.)

People love personal service. They often long for the return of the days when they could walk into a deli and have the familiar and friendly butcher tell them that the corned beef they like so much just arrived. A good specialty store builds its success on a sales staff that keeps detailed records of customers' purchases and notifies them if the store has another item they might like. It is all well and good for customers to share that kind of personal information face-to-face with a real-life person they trust, but sending that same information into cyberspace where it will be shared with agents, third parties, and unnamed marketing partners is quite another matter. More trade-offs: friends versus strangers, face-to-face versus faceless relationships, trust versus skepticism.

Two forces are driving this dilemma. The first is the rapidly growing and changing technology. Even just a decade ago, the collection of data about customers' personal lives was not possible. At that time, customers at least knew if they were divulging intimate details of their lives. Today, they do it without their knowing. The second force is the growing distance between buyer and seller. Long ago, transactions were consummated in person because there was no alternative. Now, buying and selling can be done by mail, telephone, and even computer. With each advancement, buyers become more separated or perhaps even alienated from sellers. Neither of these forces shows any signs of abatement.

It is not just buyers who are forced to make trade-offs, but sellers too. The data that companies collect—for example, information about preferences between two products or about how customers move the mouse on their computers—are valuable in the aggregate. But if marketers link that data with specific individuals, the data's value increases many times over. As the *Post* article states, "Personal data is pure gold for advertisers ... and the Internet has opened huge opportunities for marketers at the same time it has created privacy risks for consumers" (Irwin 2001, p. E1). The operative word here is "gold." So marketers must choose between maximizing the value of their shareholders' investment and respecting the privacy rights of their customers. It is the now-familiar trade-off between economics and ethics.

The debate over privacy often comes down to whether marketers give customers the opportunity to opt in to their service or merely to opt out. Should marketers offer customers the choice of whether to send personal information after ensuring that customers have all the facts about how their information will be used? Or can marketers just allow those customers to limit the use of their personal information if the customers take the trouble to read the fine print of privacy policies and go through the rigmarole of notifying the company? The answers to these questions will depend on yet another trade-off: Do marketers really respect the privacy of the majority of consumers, or do they hide behind the fact that the same majority willingly divulges personal information and only a vocal minority expresses concern?

Finally, marketers confront two other trade-offs that are addressed throughout these essays. First, they must choose between government regulation and self-regulation. Regarding the issue of Internet privacy, the federal government has relied so far on companies to regulate themselves. That is changing, however, because the results have been less than satisfactory. The Federal Trade Commission has stepped in to protect children under 13 years of age and customers of online financial services. The more marketers succumb to the "gold" in their customers' personal information and the more they rely solely on opt-out provisions, the more the vocal minority will insist that the government step in and set standards and policies.

Second, marketers must decide between cooperative and adversarial relationships with their customers. Will marketers treat their customers as valuable partners and seek to increase both parties' benefits from transactions? Or will they approach each marketing decision as a zero-sum game: They can benefit only by taking something away from their customers? Perhaps I should not be impatient and expect that this last trade-off will be resolved anytime soon: It is a troublesome question that has gone unresolved for thousands of years.

1. Do opt-out provisions satisfy marketers' ethical obligations to customers, or must marketers offer opt-in provisions?

2. If customers willingly divulge personal data to marketers, what obligations do marketers have regarding the use of that data?

3. Visit the LifeMinders Web site, read the company's privacy policies, and comment on whether its customers are adequately protected.

INAPPROPRIATE MARKETING

In the same issue, Jacquelyn Ottman, who wrote a column for *Marketing News* on Green Marketing in the 1990s, describes the lengthy and complex process by which the Federal Trade Commission reviews and revises its Guidelines for Environmental Marketing Terms. According to Ottman (1996, p. 13), the purpose of these guidelines is to reduce deception and "customer confusion about green claims" and "promote national consistency."

Over the past ten years, with the consuming public becoming more concerned about environmental problems, marketers have rushed to take advantage of this new opportunity to promote their products. Claims such as "recyclable," "nontoxic," "energy efficient," "ozone friendly," "all natural," and "not tested on animals" began appearing on cans and boxes, sometimes with little or no justification.

A budding competition has developed between sellers of eco-seals such as the "Green Seal," which is an environmental version of the old Good Housekeeping Seal of Approval. In many cases, there are no acceptable standards for testing such claims. Under these circumstances, there is the tendency for competition to sink to the lowest ethical level. If one marketer uses the label "reusable" or "environmentally friendly," whether or not the claim has any substance, there is pressure on all competitors to beat that claim. No wonder the public has been confused.

I join Semon and Ottman in identifying two important themes. First, it is difficult for marketers to exercise restraint. By their very nature, marketers are optimistic, aggressive, quick to take the initiative, and eager to get a jump on the competition. Invariably, this leads to ethics abuses sooner or later. As much as business rails against government regulations, this lack of self-restraint makes them inevitable. If marketers cannot or will not police themselves, then some federal or state agency—or both, in the case of environmental labeling—must step in and protect the public from overzealous marketing tactics. Governmental controls become the only solution to prevent consumer confusion, not to mention outright fraud.

Another possibility to protect consumers, maintain their confidence, and forestall more government regulation is an ethics-standards board representing the marketing profession. The legal and medical professions have such boards, and something of this sort will be absolutely essential if marketing, and business management more generally, is ever to become a true profession. To be effective, such boards must have adequate authority to police the members of the profession and penalize offenders.

Second, the buyer is almost always vulnerable to the seller in the marketplace. Technology, in its many wondrous forms, has outpaced the learning ability of even sophisticated buyers, so they no longer have the skill to judge advertising claims and marketing pitches effectively. This problem applies to the average supermarket shopper who buys a can of insect repellent labeled "No CFCs," as well as the experienced marketing executive who buys research services. Neither of these buyers has the knowledge necessary to judge these claims about the product or service. Adam Smith's classic situation in which glove maker and glove purchaser came together with approximately equal standing and power in the market is a quaint relic of the past. Today, consumers are at the mercy of marketers for the vast majority of their purchases and have only limited resources, knowledge, and skill with which to judge the claims being made.

There is every likelihood that these trends will continue and that products and services will become increasingly complex and, therefore, difficult for consumers to evaluate. Thus, it becomes increasingly important for marketers to consider the moral dimension of their strategic and tactical decisions. Government regulations and guidelines may be inevitable, but they can be held to a minimum by conscientious marketing behavior.

Moral awareness and ethical analysis must be incorporated into the mainstream of marketing literature, teaching, and learning, not pigeonholed in a separate, usually elective business school course. A regard for ethical behavior deserves to be—it must be—an important aspect of everyday life and practice in marketing.

1. Identify some of the moral dilemmas that marketing researchers face.

2. What is wrong, if anything, with marketers' use of phrases such as "nontoxic," "energy efficient," or "all natural?"

33

Cloning and the Responsibility of Marketers

In 1997, the startling—some thought frightening—news came out of Scotland about the cloning of Dolly, a sheep, which was an accomplishment previously thought impossible. Ian Wilmut, lead scientist on the project, noted at the time that there was no reason, in theory, that the same or a similar process could not be used to clone humans, though he adamantly opposed the idea. Five years later, although there is overwhelming opposition to cloning humans in the United States, scientists elsewhere are beginning to develop the process. I am absolutely certain that this will become a moral question for marketers sooner than expected.

Only 25 years ago, the National Academy of Sciences sponsored a conference to discuss the benefits and risks of novel gene-splicing techniques. Speakers were all but drowned out by participants in the overflowing crowd who chanted, "We will not be cloned." The mayor of Cambridge, Mass., in leading a citizens' rally to protest the expansion of a genetic engineering laboratory on the Harvard University campus, warned of "seven-foot tall monsters emerging from the Boston sewers" (see Yoxen 1983).

In the mid-1980s, Advanced Genetic Sciences, a small, high-tech start-up company in California, was refused a permit to spray genetically engineered bacteria on strawberry fields to prevent frost damage to the fruit. This would have been the first time a genetically altered product was released into the atmosphere, but there were too many concerns at the time that such substances would get out of control, reproduce wildly, and cause unpredictable damage. Today, genetically engineered products are used routinely in many agricultural applications. Some critics still warn the public about unforeseen dangers, but the majority of the public seems unconcerned.

Some genetically manipulated products, in contrast, still have not been accepted by the public. Bovine somatotropin (BST), a genetically engineered hormone, can increase the milk production of dairy cows. Although BST has been approved for use by the Food and Drug Administration, various activist groups have succeeded in preventing the use of the product by threatening to boycott any supermarket that sells milk from cows treated with the hormone.

Within days of the announcement from Scotland about Dolly, *BusinessWeek* devoted its cover story to "The Biotech Century" and predicted that in the next decade, the payoff for cloning would be "immense" (Hamilton 1998). With immense payoffs in sight, can marketers be far behind?

The problem goes beyond genetic engineering. It involves the social acceptance and accommodation of breakthrough scientific discoveries. More than 50 years and two generations have passed since the first splitting of the atom, yet there is still strong social opposition to nuclear energy. Regardless of the merit of the concerns that anti-nuclear groups raise, there is no question that the initial promise of energy "too cheap to meter" has not materialized. We have the technological ability to produce cheap energy, but we are a long way from understanding all the social consequences. The marketing of nuclear energy is thwarted by social concerns.

The memory power of computers has been growing at a truly astonishing speed and has been bringing in its wake commercial applications that make people's lives more comfortable and productive. This has enabled marketers to store and access extraordinary amounts of information about customers, presumably to serve them better. Yet when Lotus and Equifax began selling the names, addresses, incomes, and spending patterns of 120 million people in a product named "Marketplace Household" at such a price that even small businesses could afford to use it to develop well-targeted, profitable mailing lists, there was such a strong social outcry that the companies scrapped their plans and their product. New England Telephone and Blockbuster Inc. also ran into opposition to their plans to sell their mailing lists and were forced to back down.

Now that sheep can be cloned, is it not inevitable that, if it proves feasible to clone humans, there will be a market for cloning services? Grieving parents might clone a dying child, for example. What role will or should marketers play? Should the government impose constraints, or should marketers impose constraints on themselves? Referring to the sheep-cloning news, a bioethicist from the University of Pennsylvania posed the problem succinctly: "It's an incredible development. Unfortunately, we don't have the legal or ethical basis to handle it yet" (see Hamilton 1998). Twenty-seven years after the birth of genetic engineering, society is still searching for that basis.

In 1975, shortly after scientists discovered the technology for moving DNA from one cell to another, the world's leading molecular biologists did an absolutely extraordinary thing. Aware that their work posed potential risks and that various groups opposed genetic engineering on moral grounds, they voluntarily imposed a moratorium on their work until the National Institutes of Health could develop protocols that would answer many, if not all, of the questions being raised. National Institutes of Health provided a seal of legitimacy to the work, and the result was an orderly unfolding of biotechnology research and development that minimized social and ethical opposition.

Are marketers capable of such restraint? A precipitous rush to market cloning services or a similar biotechnology minefield could lead to disaster. At best, it could lead to government regulation; at worst, adverse public opinion could lead to a ban on the product or service from the market entirely. Perhaps the twenty-first century will be "The Biotech Century." Perhaps the cloning of vital organs, other body parts, or entire human beings is in the near future. My hope is that marketers will not be so dazzled by the profit potential that they will neglect the moral dimension of such developments. I hope that marketers, like the scientists in 1975, will be willing to pause and help develop guidelines that will inspire a greater degree of social confidence in their work.

1. Should marketers bear any of the responsibility for gaining social approval of new technological products and services?

2. Is it marketers' jobs to promote controversial products and sway the public toward accepting them, or should marketers be neutral and wait for public acceptance?

34

Guess? Ads Cross the Line Between Fashion Art and Pornography

This essay first ran in Marketing News *on October 21, 1996. Rather than update the essay by changing the tenses of a few verb forms, I thought it might be more interesting to include it in its original form. Readers will agree, I believe, that similar ads to those discussed are no less prevalent today.*

As a former retailer of women's fashion apparel for many years, I still look forward each spring and fall to the *New York Times* fashion supplements. In late August, the fashion section arrived, and I plunged eagerly into it looking for what designers and retailers had in store for women this fall.

I turned only a few pages, however, before I was stopped by the two-page spread from Guess? jeans. Seldom had I seen such pornography being presented as fashion advertising. On the left page, a girl who looks to be 14 or 15 years of age is in a theater seat wearing jeans and a tank top with her legs spread wide apart, her hair disheveled, a coy smirk, and an empty popcorn and soft-drink cup carefully positioned between her legs to suggest sexual coupling.

On the right page, the same girl is shown closer to the camera, but the focus is softer and suggests a dreamy, hallucinatory mood. Her pouty mouth is open slightly, and between her teeth she is holding part of a necklace, which, I assume, is an erotic symbol. She is in a semireclined pose, and the camera angle is such that the focus of the ad is on her breasts, only barely covered by a cropped tank top.

This ad is pornography, pure and simple, worthy of *Penthouse* or *Hustler*. I recognize the danger of, or difficulty in, one person interpreting any art form, and fashion photography is certainly an art form. What I deem pornographic may not seem so to another person. I leave it to my readers to judge for themselves, on the basis of their tastes and values.

Didn't this controversy occur less than a year ago, when Calvin Klein ran a series of suggestive ads using youthful-looking models? That effort ended in Klein canceling the ads under heavy social pressure and offering a public apology. Why would Guess? attempt to "outporn" Calvin Klein? Why make such a concerted and expensive effort to come as close as possible to the bounds of acceptability without feeling the censor's scissors?

Let me go further. In neither ad is the merchandise shown in any detail or with any clarity. There is nothing distinctive about either the jeans or the tank top, at least as shown in the ad. The items could be from any of hundreds of apparel manufacturers.

So what is the ad designed to do? Is the message that wearing Guess? clothing will lead to some unimaginably erotic experience? At the very least, the ad's creators must hope to cut through the clutter of all the other ads in the supplement by using sex to direct the reader's attention to the Guess? name and logo in the most erotic and startling ad in the magazine.

Who is the target for these ads? Surely, only a limited number of teenage girls nationwide pore over the pages of the *New York Times* fashion supplements. The principal readers are the thousands of retailers, fashion buyers, and merchandise managers who treat these semiannual supplements like a bible. To get their attention, it is important to cut through the clutter, but the message is that Guess? will break the rules, which is just what teenage consumers are seeking. Here are two eye-catching, suggestive ads that can be used as posters on retail floors. The message to retailers: Young girls will flock to your stores, so load up with Guess? apparel for the season.

There is plenty of blame to go around for breaching the bounds of acceptable standards in these ads. To be flamboyant, exciting, youthful, and even daring is wonderful. But to glorify the tawdry side of sex is a harmful message to send to teenagers. It is wrong to do that.

I fault Guess? of course. One of the ads points out in small print that a member of the family that controls Guess? is the art director. Perhaps his ego has surpassed his good business judgment and his good taste. I fault *The New York Times* for running the ads. Yes, censorship is difficult. To draw the line between what is merely suggestive and what is harmful pornography is a tough job, but the newspaper that, with some justification, claims to being the finest in the world should not shrink from the task.

I fault the creators at the advertising agency who helped prepare the ads. Is their well of creativity so shallow and so limited that resorting to pornography is the only way of attracting readers and viewers for their clients? I fault the retailers that will use the ads as free promotional tools, and I fault the retailers, especially the large and powerful fashion stores, that continue to buy from Guess? without at least registering a protest.

Seeing such ads in a fine publication like *The New York Times* is discouraging to me. But not all marketers make irresponsible and immoral decisions. If marketers are to improve their reputations and ethical standards, however, it is important that they speak out. It is important that they celebrate the decent and reject the vulgar.

1. Do the ads for Guess? apparel go beyond the bounds of social acceptability? Why, or why not? If not, what are the proper bounds?

2. Even if *The New York Times* had refused to run these ads, presumably some other newspapers would have done so. What person or agency should bear the responsibility of censoring truly unacceptable reading and viewing material?

3. Is an objection to these ads mere prudishness, or given the very real problems of increasing teenage sexual activity—sexually transmitted diseases, for example—are there substantive social and moral problems involved?

35

Is Greed a Necessary Ingredient for Success in Business?

One of the maxims for success that Raymond A. Mason, chief executive officer of Legg, Mason, Inc., offered in a commencement address at Mount Saint Mary's College was, "Don't be greedy." Whether one considers greed a sin or not—it is, after all, one of the classic "seven deadly sins"—surely greed is one of the least attractive human characteristics. It would be hard to find any system of values in the world today, religious or secular, that did not warn against greed—except business and, specifically, marketing. What then should business majors and marketing students in particular make of Mr. Mason's advice?

Students are taught that business is a highly competitive struggle. "It's a jungle out there," they hear. Therefore, marketing students learn appropriate tactics for survival in a jungle and that the only way a company can grow is to take market share away from the competition. Admired business leaders often preach the gospel of "wanting it all" and never being satisfied, and sometimes they extol greed specifically. How are students expected to reconcile these mixed messages?

Consider the examples that some of the most successful and esteemed marketing organizations set. Nike pushed its market share in the United States to more than 40%, which left its arch rival Reebok trailing badly. Then, Nike lost some of its gains to Adidas and New Balance. As a counterattack, Nike pursued more of the world's soccer-shoe business, in which Adidas held a decided edge, instead of merely dominating the basketball shoe market. As an opening shot in this battle, Nike paid an unprecedented $200 million for the right to sponsor the Brazilian national soccer team, overwhelming Adidas and grabbing the sponsorship. Nike's competitors, especially Adidas, screamed for a red card foul.

For Coca-Cola, being the world's best-known brand name and the largest soft drink producer is nowhere near enough. Although the company's growth has slowed recently, it is struggling to regain its hefty annual increases by saturating every retail outlet and convincing every fountain and restaurant in the United States, and then the world, to serve Coca-Cola products. No country is too small, no town is too remote to escape the relentless pursuit of Coke's marketing team. The joke around the Atlanta headquarters used to be that the company would not rest until the "C" on all faucets signifies a Coke spigot.

Philip Morris is another example of a company that pushes competitive practices to or beyond acceptable limits, even in the face of ongoing investigations by the Federal Trade Commission. Several years ago, the company, which manufactures Marlboro, was fighting off a seemingly endless string of product liability lawsuits and dealing with attorneys general from more than 30 states who sought to recover billions of dollars in medical costs due to smoking. At the same time, it was also focusing on getting more exposure for its products at convenience stores, gas stations, liquor stores, and the other tens of thousands of retail outlets that sell cigarettes. Philip Morris introduced its "exclusivity program," which rewarded wholesalers and retailers that agreed not to install permanent displays that featured its competitors' products. Clearly, the company is not content with its roughly 50% of the U.S. cigarette market; it wants more.

Even the health care industry is not immune to marketing greed, which for some firms in the industry includes brass-knuckle hardball marketing tactics, hospital takeovers, and large bonuses for managers who meet their financial goals and increase revenues from patients.

What should be made of such examples? Are these companies no better than playground bullies, or are they business community heroes because of their unwavering focus on greater market share, revenues, and profits and their willingness to do whatever it takes to become and remain number one? Small companies that produce and sell athletic shoes, soft drinks, or cigarettes must climb into the ring with Nike, Coca-Cola, or Philip Morris. Few can survive the pummeling they take. There is a real need for a clearer set of rules to define acceptable behavior in marketing; focusing on the moral dimension of marketing is a good place to start.

Society must assign greater responsibility to companies of greater size. Society should expect more restraint and ethical behavior from corporate giants than what they have been exercising. In addition, industry associations and the government should monitor heavyweights more closely and penalize them more harshly when they break the rules. It is true that these corporate giants are providing most of the muscle that drives the economy: creating jobs, investing billions of dollars, and so forth. That should not let them off the hook in either the moral or the legal sense. Along with their steady growth, they should be exemplars of sensitivity to the needs of the larger business community and of the greater society. Too often they have been examples of bullying and greed.

Finally, despite the many complaints about the heavy hand of government intervention, business affairs could not take place without some level of government control. But government need not be the only arbiter of fair play. Consumers give or withhold their approval of a company's marketing and competitive tactics with each purchase they make. They should factor in the manufacturer's social performance with the price and quality of the product before making their purchases. Large, powerful, and active consumer advocacy organizations can effectively publicize, reject, and penalize the low blows and rabbit punches thrown by some large corporations.

Raymond Mason was right. Corporations and the managers who control them need not subscribe to greed to be successful in business. Corporate executives can set reasonable rules for competition, and companies can and must abide by them. It *is* possible to reach sensible economic goals and at the same time honor ethical values. Marketers *can* achieve both profitability and fairness.

1. If a company were to play by a less aggressive set of rules—perhaps even sacrificing a small portion of its market share and profitability—would it do a disservice to its shareholders? In other words, is greed necessary?

2. Should there be any limits to competitive practices?

3. Are there any social or economic problems associated with the domination of more and more industries by a few giant firms?

36

Marketing Tantra: Over the Line or Harmless Nonsense?

Take a large portion of New Age psychobabble, mix in an even larger portion of old fashioned sex, and you have Tantra. What marketer wouldn't love to get his or her hands on such a potent product and promote it aggressively?

Not long ago *The Wall Street Journal* reported that Tantra, a 4000-year-old quasi-religious doctrine and practice, has its "new wave of entrepreneurs" eager to market this mixture of sex and hokum to Americans who are "shedding their inhibitions and willing to treat their sex lives like their tennis games—as something to be worked on preferably with the help of a pro" (Nomani 1998, p. A1). The newspaper goes on to say that Tantra's original Sanskrit texts promoted "ritual copulation.... Women were goddesses meant to be worshipped by men on the path to mutual cosmic bliss."

Clearly this is worth further investigation. Besides, Tantra seems to have gained some respectability. Some colleges and universities, including the University of Virginia, have begun teaching Tantra theory in their religious studies programs. To learn more about this fascinating field, I turned to what I consider the best source of all New Age information, the Internet. Two clicks brought me to the first of 1,565,908 matches: The Church of Tantra. Here I learned that the "ritual satisfaction of lust" would help me realize "the unity of flesh and spirit, of the human and the divine" (www.tantra.org). Furthermore, I learned that Tantra borrows from many traditions including Hindu, Buddhist, Taoist, Native American, Quodoshka, Wiccan, African, Polynesian, and Christian Gnostic.

Continued clicking brought me to a Web site featuring several stylized ancient Indian artworks that depict pornographic poses and sexual positions. I declined an invitation to join the Church of Tantra, but I did accept the offer to peruse the church's eSensuals catalog, which features an extraordinary collection of sex enhancers including bawdy butter, a rabbit-fur massage mitt, and a crystal egg for vaginal weight-lifting.

Well! There seemed to be plenty of material here for anyone interested in marketing ethics. Any practice that promotes "polyamory— seeking of Tantric bliss through multiple partners" (Nomani 1998)— would seem ripe for moral examination. We might ask first what harm is being done. After all, the buyers are adults who consent to purchase not only "lust dust" but also weekend seminars priced from $300 to $600. Workshops in Maui, for example, allow participants to swim with the dolphins, and there is even a Tantric vacation seminar in Bali for $3,100. I read no reports of dissatisfaction from those who have paid to learn how to have "sacred sex" among lighted candles and soothing music. Perhaps the buyers are getting exactly what they hoped for, in which case there may be no harm done at all.

Have these buyers been misled, though? The purveyors of Tantra, according to the *Journal* story, seem to be a strange and questionable group of religious or quasi-religious leaders. There is the Indian, Osho, who was deported for immigration fraud. There is Corynne Clarchick, who gave up running an escort service, renamed herself Dr. Corynna Clark, and began promoting her Tantra-training firm Temple of the Goddess. If the buyers of balms, books, sex seminars, and dolphin swims really are looking for sexual healing and excitement, perhaps they do not care about the theological qualifications and training of Osho and Clark. Perhaps the market has worked admirably well in matching buyers with the appropriate sellers.

"There's a sucker born every minute," P.T. Barnum was famous for saying. Out of context, the quote sounds manipulative and malicious. But when people go to the circus or to see a magician perform, they know what to expect. They want to be amazed, entertained, and, yes, even deceived. People voluntarily suspend their disbelief every time they visit a movie theater or the stage. Perhaps Tantra seekers do not really expect their guides in the search to be true religious leaders. They may be getting exactly what they pay for.

I grant that with the promotion and sale of Tantra, there is the *potential* for harm. It is quite possible that innocent and naive people will suffer emotional and psychological distress. It is quite possible that there could be harm done to society in general if Tantra moved toward the mainstream. There is also, however, the possibility that some Tantra seekers and participants will gain some benefit, whether real or perceived. I am the least likely person to embrace any sort of New Age fad, but it is usually impossible to prove scientifically that the claims of any such practices are false.

So, I say that if Hawaiian Goddess Inc. and scores of would-be swamis and sexual coaches use Tantra to cash in on the thriving feel-good industry, so be it. If they use the latest marketing concepts—niche marketing, brand extensions, penetration pricing, e-commerce, and strategies to capture market share—to hawk their wares, it just goes to show what a powerful and inclusive discipline marketing is.

Unless Tantra and its aftershocks cause real harm to individuals or communities, I am willing to regard it more with humor than horror. So far, the story sounds to me like a small group of adults, looking for out-of-the-ordinary forms of entertainment and experience. They may have outgrown the circus, but they still want to be amazed, shocked, and pleasantly deceived. Every day there is affirmation of Barnum's famous quip.

1. Under what circumstances would the marketing of Tantra be immoral?

2. Should promotions of and references to Tantra be banned from the Internet because it is easily accessible by young children?

37

Political Ads and Demeaning the Competition

Marketing, as both an art and a science, is most often thought about in the context of the world of business, the for-profit world. However, in textbooks and lectures, students are reminded that marketing concepts are also essential for nonprofit organizations (e.g., the Salvation Army, hospitals, churches), government bodies, and especially political candidates.

Early in the 1996 Iowa Republican primary, Bob Dole seemed unbeatable. Then Steve Forbes, to almost everyone's surprise, rose rapidly in the polls and actually became the front runner shortly before the caucuses. Later in the campaign, Forbes declined in the standings as rapidly as he had risen. Forbes's success and failure were attributed to two factors: the overwhelming amount of advertising he paid for out of his own pocket and the extraordinarily negative nature of the ads. The pundits reported that Iowa's conservative majority finally became fed up with the barrage of negative ads Forbes directed at all his opponents, and especially at Dole.

A few of the ads, viewers were told, contained falsehoods. Many of the ads stretched the truth beyond reasonable limits, and almost all of them were mean-spirited. Forbes's poor showing in the caucuses suggests that in the end, this strategy was counterproductive. The heavy reporting and discussion of the negative ads may even have hurt Forbes in the later New Hampshire primary in which he finished a distant fourth.

Why do political contests turn nasty so often? Common wisdom is that, like it or not, negative advertising "moves the numbers," which is political jargon that means a political candidate's standings in the polls will rise if he or she lashes out at the opposition. This bit of political wisdom might have changed after the 1996 elections; unfortunately, though, negative campaign advertising is still common. Presumably, there is a lesson here for political candidates, but what are the lessons for marketers? Is there a counterpart to this story in the for-profit business world?

The increasingly common use of comparative advertising comes to mind: An advertiser directly refers to the competition and demeans its product, which in theory elevates the advertiser's own offering. There was a time when this practice was taboo. It was considered unseemly, inappropriate, and counterproductive. Any mention of a competitor's product, no matter in what context, was giving unnecessary recognition to that product and the brand name. Why would any company use its valuable and limited advertising budget to even mention the name of a competing brand?

Now, the practice is relatively common. Pepsi uses the approach to poke fun at Coke. In one ad, delivery drivers for the two companies sit down together late at night in a diner. Each tastes the other's drink. The Pepsi driver nods politely after tasting the Coke and gives it back. But the Coke driver likes his first sip of Pepsi so much that he won't give it back. Another Pepsi ad shows a Coke driver trying furtively to sneak a Pepsi out of a convenience store cooler without being noticed, but the Pepsi cans come flooding out, and he is mightily embarrassed. Also on television, Chevrolet lightheartedly makes direct comparisons between its cars and similar models from Ford and Toyota using a split-screen technique.

Perhaps the most memorable and controversial examples of this genre are the Visa ads that slyly demean American Express. After showing an ideal couple enjoying the natural beauty of the Monterey Peninsula or the charm of Capri, the ad tells viewers to bring their sunglasses and their Visa cards because a particular inn or restaurant won't accept American Express.

American Express has also used comparative advertising and stirred up controversy. In 1992, Visa paid millions of dollars to be an official sponsor of the Barcelona Olympic games, and American Express retaliated with a guerilla marketing counterattack by assuring television viewers that they did not need a visa (Visa?) to visit Barcelona. American Express hoped that using Barcelona in its ads would create the false impression that American Express, too, was a sponsor of the games.

Is there a moral problem here? Probably not, if this is as far as things go. The comparative product advertising mentioned here is mostly lighthearted and amusing. The Visa–American Express standoff is a somewhat testy public display of a bitter, behind-the-scenes battle in which Visa is fighting to protect its investment. The potential problem is whether marketers will push this practice too far. Will advertisers be tempted to go beyond humor to demean a competitor's product and perhaps stretch the truth in the process?

The lesson from the political battles of 1996 is this: Marketers must be wary of using strident attacks on their competition. The public will accept and even enjoy lighthearted references to the competition. However, if ads are perceived as bitter and mean and if marketers stretch the truth in putting down their opponents or praising their own products to "move the numbers" of market share in their favor, they will suffer the same chilly rejection that Steve Forbes suffered in the winter primaries of Iowa and New Hampshire.

1. What, if anything, is unethical about disparaging a competitor's product?

2. What are the similarities and dissimilarities between comparative ads in business and in politics?

38

The Influence of Corporate Money on Nonprofits

A few years ago, two stories appeared in *The Washington Post* that were unrelated in subject matter but touched on a common ethical question: To what extent can and should corporate donations to nonprofit organizations influence the activities of those groups?

The first article reported that Nike had struck a deal with Ohio State University (OSU) under which the athletic shoe manufacturer would pay the university $9.25 million over five years for the exclusive privilege of supplying all its male and female athletes and coaches with shoes and apparel. A total of $5 million, $1 million for each year of the agreement, would provide actual footwear and clothing; $500,000 would go toward marketing; and the balance of $3.75 million would be split among the coaching staff.

The second article announced that Nissan Motor Corp. USA would donate $100,000 to the National Association for the Advancement of Colored People (NAACP) in addition to a previous gift of $50,000. The article vaguely explained how the money would be spent: outreach to minority communities, voter registration, education, and recruitment.

There is a considerable difference in the amounts of money involved in these two situations, but in both cases corporations made payments to nonprofit organizations that were beyond the scope of their normal operations. There is nothing necessarily wrong or even questionable about this, but it is worth examining further.

The first question that comes to mind is, What were the motives for each corporation? Nike's motive is probably clear enough: Sponsorship is a form of advertising that guarantees that the company's Swoosh logo will appear on the uniforms, jerseys, shoes, and warm-up jackets of every OSU athlete and coach. Ohio State is a big, prominent athletic school with lots of television exposure. Five million dollars may prove to be a good "buy," depending on how much television time the university receives over the five years of the deal. Appearances in postseason games such as the Rose Bowl or the NCAA basketball's Final Four would sweeten the deal for Nike. This expenditure by Nike is more of an advertising buy than a donation, though the money is going to the university.

What about ethical problems? There is certainly room to question the payment to the coaches. Is this a form of bribery? Accepting big sums from a sponsor can influence the coaches' and athletic directors' decisions as to which opponents to include on the schedule and which players to play. A sponsor is interested in these matters because they affect how large a television audience could be anticipated. The administrators and trustees of OSU undoubtedly had mixed feelings about the arrangement. On the one hand, it is a cost-free way to keep top-notch coaches at the university. On the other hand, the coaches may feel they are working for Nike and not OSU.

What about the agreement that the players would wear Nike shoes and apparel? The Athletic Director at Ohio State commented, "We've got so many signs all over the place now, one more sign [the Swoosh on the uniforms] won't make a difference." So the players and coaches become signboards that advertise Nike, and who would be harmed by that? The players don't seem to mind. After all, Nike is the most popular brand of athletic shoe in the United States. Both Nike and OSU must be pleased with the arrangement, or they would not have agreed to it.

There is some reason to be concerned, however, about the reaction of the fans, especially the television audience. Although many viewers will not notice the logo, sponsorship can be overdone. Too many signs in the stadium and too many logos on uniforms can detract from what is supposed to be an amateur sport and turn it into one long commercial. Many fans would resent the players being turned into the human equivalent of Nascar race cars.

How far should this commercialization extend? Should high school athletes also become long-playing advertising messages? This is less likely to happen because high schools do not command huge television audiences. But the process has begun; the nose of the camel is under the tent even at the high school level, and the principle of keeping primary and secondary schools free of commercialism is at stake.

What about Little League baseball? Traditionally, local businesses have been the sponsors of Little League, providing T-shirts emblazoned with the businesses' names. By comparison, Nike's Swoosh on OSU jerseys is downright discreet.

Questionable payments to coaches aside, the ethical concerns in this commercial transaction seem minor, assuming that there is nothing hidden in the deal. Another sign or another logo does not seem to transgress any moral boundaries. If the transaction leads to undue corporate influence on the school's athletic program, however, that would be cause for worry.

The Nissan story is not so straightforward, and therefore it is more difficult to analyze. Return to the question of motive: Why did Nissan commit $150,000 to the NAACP? Perhaps it was simply a charitable gift to help strengthen one of the United States' most conservative and widely respected civil rights organizations at a time when more radical groups with divisive agendas were gaining attention. Many would deem this a worthy goal, though it is an unusual choice for a Japanese firm to make.

Perhaps the donation was less altruistic. Was there a hidden agenda, and were there strings attached to the gift? It is conceivable that Nissan was buying the right to be heard by this venerable African American organization to help ensure labor peace. This goal might well pass an ethical screen also, but the problem is that Nissan did not state its purposes publicly.

Philosophers have debated for millennia whether there is such a thing as pure altruism. Of more immediate concern, however, is whether a corporation should make charitable donations and to what extent those donations should further the corporation's obvious purposes (making and selling cars or shoes), at least indirectly. Currently, there is widespread agreement that charitable donations—for example, corporate support for a community symphony orchestra—pass an ethical screen, because a corporation has obligations to the community in which it operates in addition to its shareholders. Such donations also pass a legal screen, because support for the orchestra can redound to the benefit of the corporation by making the community more attractive and better able to maintain a qualified workforce for its corporate citizens.

Money is a form of power and influence, of this there can be no doubt. When federal, state, and local government funding for education, the arts, entertainment, advocacy, and sports is stretched to the very limit, corporations are expected to help fill these community needs. Yet, gifts from a corporation to a nonprofit group are, or are perceived to be, suspect. Of course, there is some historical basis for this skepticism. Whether it is Nike influencing the athletic schedules at OSU, Pepsi controlling the distribution of soft drinks at Penn State in exchange for a handsome contribution, or one of the giant oil companies contributing to an environmental group, the public has reason to view such gifts with a jaundiced eye. How to fulfill this expanded social mandate but avoid the abuse of power that can be so tempting is a narrow tightrope corporate managers must learn to walk. The transparency of purpose and the absence of hidden agendas are good places to start.

1. What limits should society, through government regulation or other means, place on corporate sponsorship and involvement in sports?

2. Should corporate donations such as Nissan's gift to the NAACP require more public explanation and review?

Calvin Klein Ads Were a Mistake

What observer of marketing ethics could pass up the opportunity to comment on the ads for Calvin Klein jeans that ran a few years ago? Seldom does an advertising campaign stir up such controversy and opposition that the president of the United States feels obligated to weigh in with a moral judgment. It may be ironic that this particular president, Bill Clinton, commented publicly on any moral issue. In any case, his judgment was simple and straightforward—no caveats; no ifs, ands, or buts; no "on the one hand...." For President Clinton, the ads were just plain wrong.

The ads in question were in a portfolio of fashion magazine advertisements that featured young models in sexy and suggestive poses, undressed to varying degrees and in various ways so that the Calvin Klein underwear was casually exposed. There was a companion television spot with lewd, voyeuristic comments from an off-camera male director to the young female model, and there was the obligatory Times Square billboard with a reclining, pouty waif tantalizing Manhattan pedestrians.

Over the years, Calvin Klein has built a reputation for pushing the envelope in his ads for jeans, underwear, and perfume. Beginning with the Brooke Shields's slightly naughty, "Nothing comes between me and my Calvins," the designer invariably has searched for new, avant-garde ways, some of which incorporate totally nude bodies, to shock readers and grab their attention. So why did these ads cause more controversy than usual? Why did some magazine editors refuse to run them?

The answer lies in two words: child pornography. Society tolerates a considerable amount of sex in entertainment and advertising, more with every passing decade, but it draws the line well short of child pornography. Even the most avid free-speech activists, who will go to the barricades to defend nude dancing and X-rated films as expressions of free speech, decry the use of children in these media. The ongoing controversy of sexual content on the Internet focuses primarily on the peril to children, according to a *Time* magazine cover story titled "Cyberporn."

With this advertising campaign, Klein and his creative staff stepped over the line from sex to sleaze. He and others have produced sexier ads that feature beautiful nude or semi-nude bodies and have done a wonderful job of creating product awareness without falling into the category of pornography. This series, however, creates a calculated sense of degeneracy and a feeling of unwholesomeness. Most of all, there was an emphasis on youth. Klein touched a sore spot in the American psyche, and when he eventually pulled the ads, it did little to salve the wound. The FBI reportedly investigated the true ages of the models to determine if child pornography laws had been breached. Klein assured the public that the models claimed to be 18 years or older. Whatever the facts on that question, what is important is that the public perceived the models to be children, and in his own words, Klein intended the ads to appeal to children.

These ads fail to pass both traditional frameworks for screening ethical problems. First, the result of running these ads was a greater cost to society than a benefit. The ad's apparent affirmation of sordid and permissive conduct on the part of teenagers outweighs any marginal profit Klein might have received. (His firm put together a quite different replacement campaign that was no less effective than the offensive campaign.) Second, the ads violated important rights and principles. Society has a right, indeed an obligation, to protect its children from pornography, even if that means placing some limits on Klein's rights to free speech and artistic expression.

This is not a call for censorship, or at least not for government or third-party censorship. Klein and all advertisers must make their own decisions as to how far to push the boundaries of sex that society will accept, and each magazine publisher must make the choice of whether to print the ads.

Is there a generational gap at work in this example? My undergraduate students, who are perhaps overexposed to the excesses of Britney Spears, J.Lo, and the explicit depictions of sex in the "gangsta rap" music they crave, mostly had a ho-hum attitude toward the ads. Their responses to my questions fell into three categories: "I've seen a lot worse," "They have to do it to make money," and "So what's the big deal?" These are sincere thoughts, perhaps, but hardly serious ethical analysis.

People of honesty, intelligence, and goodwill can disagree on the subject of moral standards, but I side with President Clinton and label these ads as "wrong;" that is, they represent a poor ethical decision. A related question should be asked, however: Was running the ads a good business decision? Even the bad publicity from these ads arguably created more brand awareness, and perhaps Calvin Klein's customers and potential customers would relish nothing more than to challenge publicly accepted standards. Surely, that would be only a short-term gain. Over the long run, every firm must have some level of public acceptance and legitimacy. It was poor judgment on Klein's part to misread the public's level of tolerance so badly that he crossed the line beyond sex and sensuousness to child pornography and imagined that the public would not protest strongly.

Although Klein can be criticized for running the ads, he can also be complimented for withdrawing them voluntarily. Too many sordid and pornographic advertising campaigns, just like too many dangerous products or instances of price fixing, will result in some form of government regulation. Government censorship is an unattractive and perhaps unworkable way to constrain the excesses of marketers. Timely self-restraint is far better.

1. If limits on the sexual content of advertising are necessary, should they be set by government, business, and the community acting together in some way, such as the Better Business Bureau, or simply by the workings of the free market?

2. Where do you believe those limits should be set, and why?

40

Excessive Student Drinking: Whose Responsibility?

One of the most intractable, and saddest, problems facing virtually every college and university in the United States today is excessive student drinking. All too often, the media must report stories about college students found dead of alcohol poisoning in their dormitories or in alcohol-related traffic accidents or injured in fights resulting from too much drinking at parties.

In a 2002 membership solicitation letter, Mothers Against Drunk Driving (MADD) states that in the year 2000, "9.7 million young people aged 12–20 reported drinking alcohol ... 6.6 million of them were binge drinkers and 2.1 million were heavy drinkers." In addition, MADD reports that 44% of college students engage in binge drinking, which means they down four or five drinks at a single sitting.

For anyone interested in marketing, and especially in questions of marketing ethics and corporate social responsibility, the spotlight quickly focuses on the major breweries and their marketing programs. True enough, wine and distilled spirits are involved in binge drinking but to a considerably lesser degree. Beer is the drink of choice for most college students. In addition, there are plenty of stakeholders other than the brewers.

- ✦Colleges and universities are torn between, on the one hand, providing a safe and healthy environment for their students and complying with the law and, on the other hand, recognizing the competitive pressures to accede to students' wishes for maximum freedom of choice and action. It is no surprise that some students view going off to college as their passport to freedom from parental supervision. One of the easiest symbols of this freedom is drinking.
- ✦The students' parents expect the schools to provide a safe environment, but they have done little at home to change and perhaps have contributed to the students' cavalier attitudes about drinking.

✦Advocacy groups such as MADD, Students Against Driving Drunk, and the Center for Science in the Public Interest keep up a steady drumbeat of warnings about student drinking and criticisms of the breweries. However, they have been short on constructive suggestions, and they risk seeming to push for a return to Prohibition.

✦Government bodies at both federal and state levels—legislatures, committees, and regulatory agencies—take up the issue from time to time, but they have a complex social agenda in addition to solving student drinking problems.

What is striking about all these stakeholders involved in this issue, unlike many other issues involving ethics and social responsibility, is their remarkable unanimity on one point: Excessive drinking, underage drinking, and drinking while driving must be reduced.

Students—the stakeholders at the very heart of the problem—are the lone exception. Conversations with students about the problem reveal that many of them are in denial. Their responses include: "Drinking isn't really *that* much of a problem," "Bad things [such as deaths or accidents] would have happened anyway," "There's nothing else to do," and "It's just a part of being college students."

With the exception of the students, however, all the stakeholders have the same goal: the reduction of student drinking. But what progress has been made toward reaching this goal? Why, if there is unanimity of purpose, are they not closer to a solution? What more could be done?

The major brewers have certainly not ignored the problem. Anheuser-Busch, the world's largest brewer, deserves credit for its public service advertising to promote moderation in drinking. (Let's leave aside the question of the sincerity of Anheuser's motive: whether it has run this advertising simply to forestall social criticism.) Other programs that provide advice on choosing designated drivers, training bartenders to recognize when to stop serving a customer and how to spot fake identification cards, promoting free taxi rides for those who have had too much to drink, and so forth receive less public attention. Anheuser-Busch claims to have spent more than $100 million in recent years on these efforts, and the figure for the entire industry is double or triple that amount.

The results? The beer industry proudly points out that though the problem is far from being solved, traffic-related deaths have steadily declined in recent years. This fact has hardly silenced the industry's critics, however. Advocacy groups respond that the large sums spent on preaching moderation are only a drop in the bucket compared with the amount brewers spend on promoting the pleasures of drinking.

Furthermore, MADD argues that even the moderation messages *promote* drinking by implying that moderate drinking is the norm. Designated drivers, as many young people will confirm, simply legitimize excessive drinking for everyone else. The brewers are caught in the same old bind between ethics and economics: They want to save lives and silence their critics, but they do not want to sacrifice revenue and profits.

Assume for a moment that the brewers really are serious about reducing excessive drinking, especially among college students. What more could be done? It is time to recognize three things. First, making any headway against these problems requires changing attitudes and beliefs as well as behaviors, which is a notoriously difficult task especially with teenagers, who tend to be headstrong and resist suggestions from parents and other adults.

Second, those who are working toward a significant decrease in teenage alcohol abuse have, at best, only scratched the surface. The declining number of deaths is welcome news, but the focus should be less on that accomplishment than on the still horrendous number, which constitutes a social tragedy. Third, the brewers and their critics must move beyond carping about whether the Budweiser lizards and frogs, or even Spuds MacKenzie, were implicitly meant to appeal to children to whether the ads actually led to excessive consumption. Both the industry and advocate groups are locked into positions, fighting to win relatively minor battles against each other, while the major war against a common enemy is ignored.

What is necessary is a new level of commitment on both sides, a willingness to work *together*, which they have shown little interest in so far. The obstacles to reaching such a commitment are obvious: lack of trust, suspicions, jockeying for position, and concessions. The brewers worry about losing sales and being backed into a corner in which they become the sole responsible party. Advocates worry about the perception of lying down with the "enemy."

Imagine the potential of joining the legitimacy and zeal of the advocates with the power, resources, and marketing skills of the brewers to solve a common problem and generate benefits for both sides and for society. McDonald's and the Environmental Defense Fund each took risks, put their heads together, and came up with a plan that reduced solid waste. Why shouldn't the brewers and their critics hammer out a joint program that would further reduce teenage drinking–related deaths and accidents?

1. Should the brewers bear *any* responsibility for the harm caused by selling a legal product?

2. Are the brewers' messages about moderation only a cynical attempt to establish drinking as a normal and accepted activity?

3. Whose behavior and/or policies should change? Teenagers'? Their parents'? Colleges' and universities'? The brewers'?

Internet Pornography

41

In a 2001 issue of *The Wall Street Journal*, Kara Swisher bemoans what she sees as the loss of "freedom" on the Internet. Her article, which is more an op-ed piece than a news story, responds to Yahoo!'s decision to limit its relationship with adult entertainment sites and sites that sell "adult-themed products" online. Yahoo! decided after receiving complaints from its customers that the portal would no longer facilitate the sale of material labeled "adult and erotica," nor would it accept banner ads for adult sites after the current contracts expire. Its search engine would still take Web surfers to such sites when requested, however.

Swisher (2001, p. B1) wants the Internet to remain a place where "millions of users can make legal choices in relative liberty" and suggests that easy access to adult material would prevent the Web from becoming "one big, dull shopping center/library/theme park/broadcast network." However, this is a major inconsistency because she readily accepts "ways to block children from easy access to pornographic or other age-inappropriate sites" and also "the regulation of unsolicited e-mail, or spam, full of offensive come-ons." In other words, she is unhappy that Yahoo! has set new constraints, but she is setting her own limits as to what is appropriate and what is offensive.

It is often difficult for marketers to distinguish clearly between these two categories, appropriate and offensive. There is an uneasy relationship between pornography and mainstream society and commerce. Like it or not, pornography is marginalized in U.S. culture and to greater or lesser degrees in other cultures as well. If prostitution is legal in only a handful of counties in one of the 50 states (Nevada); if stores selling adult-themed videos, books, and other products are not accepted in major shopping centers and downtown districts but instead are banished to the fringes of commercial areas; if supermarkets routinely refuse to sell *Hustler* and other sexually explicit magazines along with their wide selection of run-of-the-mill publications; if there are limits to what erotic or suggestive material is shown during prime-time television hours; and if movies and music are rated for sexual content, why shouldn't the same be expected of the Internet, which is merely the newest medium for commerce and entertainment? Is this viewpoint prudish or puritanical? Perhaps, but remember that even Swisher sets limits on what she considers appropriate Internet content.

The article also calls attention to what might be called a "maturation process." The Internet has become, rather quickly, part of the mainstream, and so it must be subject to the same questions of acceptability and appropriateness as other mainstays of the commercial and entertainment industries. Swisher (2001, p. B1) notes that America Online, in its early years, was more liberal regarding pornographic material than its stodgier competitors, CompuServe and Prodigy, but it turned away from "its racier origins as a place that tolerated free-wheeling sex chat" to accommodate a more mature and larger market. Now Yahoo! appears to have made a similar decision: To appeal to a broader spectrum of the market, it is setting more conservative limits on both the availability and the content of adult material.

This is what marketing is all about. Every marketing textbook advises marketers to search for ways to segment markets—in this example, perhaps, on the basis of what sexual material is acceptable and what is not. Then, they must target the markets that are most attractive for their business plans and tailor their product and the rest of their marketing mix to match that segment. Yahoo!, America Online, and the Internet in general are following the prescription to the letter.

This is not always an easy job, because what the target market will accept changes over time. Some decades ago, Macy's California used photography for its newspaper advertising, *except* in lingerie ads. The belief at the time was that Macy's customers would prefer not to see actual photographs of models clad only in bras, panties, or slips, at least not in daily newspapers. Sketches of models were used in the lingerie ads instead because they were thought to be more appropriate. Now, this distinction seems rather quaint and terribly dated.

What is acceptable changes rather dramatically from place to place as well as from time to time. As I noted in the "Introduction" of this section, continental Europe accepts outdoor advertising that features bare-breasted women, but the United States does not. Japan reputedly is more conservative than the United States on such matters. Marketers, especially in this age of rapidly increasing globalization, must constantly weigh what is acceptable in different cultures, religions, countries, and even regions and states. The sale of alcoholic beverages, to use another socially unacceptable product as an illustration, changes even at the county level (see Davidson 1996). Montgomery County is the only county in Maryland that requires distilled spirits to be sold in state-owned liquor stores and forbids wine and beer sales in supermarkets. Consider the effect of this policy on a firm such as Trader Joe's, the trendy "fashion food" chain, for which wine is such an important category. The firm decided to enter the Montgomery County market despite the restrictions, but its profitability in the region suffers compared with that of its other stores.

The fact that Swisher and I disagree on just where the line of appropriateness should be drawn is not the point here. What is important are three cardinal rules. First, pornography in its many forms, from merely titillating to hardcore, is one of those product categories that I have labeled "socially unacceptable." Other examples are tobacco, alcoholic beverages, firearms, and gambling. Unlike run-of-the-mill product groups such as athletic shoes or soft drinks, each of these categories contains items to which a significant part of the public objects, with varying levels of concern. For those involved in the business of pornography—racy magazines; adult-themed books, videos, and paraphernalia; night clubs featuring exotic dancers—this is a fact of life that cannot be wished away.

Second, the Internet has become mainstream. It quickly grew beyond the domain of techies and hipsters and is now used by a wide spectrum of demographic groups. As part of this maturation process, it will without question lose some of its former, freewheeling characteristics. Users cannot have it both ways. This truism applies to individual products, companies, and even entire industries: Growth requires the ability to appeal to mass markets and mass tastes. Abandoning what many consider fun, exciting, and different is a necessary part of this maturation process.

Third, marketers must, if they are doing their jobs properly, adjust their products and services and the way they are promoted to the likes and dislikes of their target markets. For Swisher, it may seem like losing an old childhood chum when Yahoo! takes a step away from its slightly kooky and irreverent origins and veers toward the mainstream. It may be disappointing for her to watch the entire Internet become more conservative regarding content or other issues such as privacy.

In the search for bigger revenues, market shares, and profits, firms are pulled toward the middle, toward mass, homogeneous tastes, toward a blander image and product line. This pull is irresistible and, for some, regrettable. As Yahoo! matures and slowly disassociates itself from lurid sites and content, surely younger and smaller portals will seize the opportunity to fill the void and become the choice for Swisher and others. The free market is a wondrous mechanism.

1. Do you think that Swisher's views regarding adult material on the Internet are hypocritical? Explain.

2. Should businesses that deal with pornography have the same rights as other businesses? For example, should they have the same opportunities to distribute their goods and services?

3. Explain why young businesses' policies might differ from those of more mature businesses.

FINAL THOUGHTS

Of Saints and Sinners

42

A few years ago, *BusinessWeek* published an editorial by Paul Craig Roberts with the attention-grabbing title, "Who Did More for Mankind, Mother Teresa or Mike Milken?" The essay was not directed at marketing ethics or even at the broader subject of business ethics, but it raised some troubling issues that are important to all managers and scholars.

At the heart of Roberts's diatribe was income inequality, which he ascribes to the normal workings of the free market and which he, therefore, accepts without question or examination. Because Milken created wealth, jobs, and income, Roberts suggests, he was a greater benefactor to humankind than Mother Teresa, who merely distributed wealth donated by philanthropists. "Yet Mother Teresa was praised for her self-sacrifice, and Milken damned for self-interest," wrote Roberts (1998, p. 28), who is a fellow at the Institute for Political Economy in Washington, D.C.

Much of the essay is rubbish. Roberts neglects to mention that Milken, along the way to creating wealth, jobs, and income was also sentenced to ten years in prison for violating securities law and spent two of those years behind bars. It was for his criminal behavior that Milken was and continues to be censured—and for which he was barred from the securities business—not his wealth-creating activity. I trust that Roberts, by his oversight, was not condoning criminal behavior as a normal, acceptable adjunct of the free market system.

In another bit of foolishness in this essay, Roberts links all American intellectuals to communism because they have raised concerns about the effects of the unfettered free market system. Whether I am an intellectual or not, I object to this McCarthy-like tactic of labeling people who hold contrary views communists. Most thoughtful people assume that such demagoguery fell out of style and practice after the 1960s, but Roberts is proof that the virus lives on.

The market as we know it is basically amoral. Nowhere in its workings does it incorporate society's sense of justice, fairness, or basic rights. For example, the market does not by itself penalize discrimination based on race or sex. In certain circumstances, the market actually fosters such discrimination. I hope that Roberts does not oppose civil rights legislation because it acts as a restraint on free market activity.

For all sorts of good reasons, society intervenes into the workings of the market to accomplish various economic and social goals. In 2001, the Federal Reserve passed a succession of interest rate cuts designed to turn around a flagging economy. Social security and civil rights legislation are other examples of government intervention. Some argue that the government intervenes too frequently; others argue that it intervenes too little. But it is folly to pretend that the so-called free market could exist without some political and social restraints. What is necessary is informed debate on specific regulations and whether the regulations' benefits outweigh the disruptions they may cause. In other words, what is needed is a straightforward, utilitarian cost/benefit analysis, but one that goes well beyond the bottom line of large corporations and considers the well-being of the entire society.

Roberts's essay addresses economists' concerns about the widening gap between the rich and the poor in the United States. Roberts (1998, p. 28) wrote that "Income inequality is not a problem, but a natural consequence of a free society." He is half right. Income disparity is indeed a natural consequence of a free market economy. However, it is wrong and dangerous to imagine it is not a problem, especially when that disparity reaches the point that it has in the United States and continues to worsen.

There are both sociopolitical and moral reasons that we should not and cannot ignore the problem of income disparity, much less cheer it on as a symbol of capitalist success. Is it unreasonable to assume that many social problems—crime, drugs, homelessness, poor education, and so on—are exacerbated by a growing anger and frustration among the poor as they witness the rich getting richer while their own situations become worse? I believe that all systems of moral or religious belief recognize that justice and fairness require the wealthy to share with those less fortunate.

Every contribution to a charity, from a modest donation in a church plate to a Carnegie-sized gift of a public library, is an example of income redistribution. So are systems of graduated income tax, Social Security, and Medicare. They may not be perfect, but they are also not part of a communist plot. Roberts should stop the name-calling and pretending that there are no problems. Then, the serious public debate over how to solve or ameliorate the problems can continue.

The United States is blessed with a marvelous economic system that has, without question, created enormous aggregate wealth and a high standard of living for many people. There will always be income disparity; the challenge is to hold it within acceptable limits. There are both pragmatic and altruistic reasons for wanting and needing to do so. But it is too serious a subject to play silly games such as comparing Mother Teresa to Michael Milken.

1. What are the advantages and disadvantages, both social and economic, of keeping income disparity within certain limits?

2. Are Michael Milken's economic achievements a legitimate excuse for his criminal activity?

3. Did Mother Teresa's work—soliciting donations to aid the poor—have damaging macroeconomic effects?

43

Overconsumption and the Responsibility of Marketers

In unguarded moments, I sometimes admit to my students and others that marketing in its crassest form is all about increasing consumption. Marketers constantly strive to sell more this year than the previous one. They look for ways to increase primary demand; they search for niches they have not yet exploited. What would their function be in an era in which consumption was limited, either by government regulation or by social constraint?

Overconsumption was the theme of the third annual Symposium on Corporate Social Responsibility at Mount Saint Mary's College, and three speakers from outside the world of business explored the subject from their respective disciplines. The first speaker, Professor Anne Ehrlich of Stanford University, addressed scientific questions about whether the earth's resources are limited and whether consumption should be restrained worldwide. This is a controversial subject that has generated heated debate for more than three decades. Conservationists make the seemingly irrefutable argument that resources are being consumed at a far faster rate than they can be replenished, that this rate is actually accelerating as the world's population grows, and that at some point (the original target date was in the middle of this century) some resources would begin growing scarce and the earth's functions would begin to deteriorate.

The so-called "cornucopia-ists" argue that such predictions have always turned out to be wrong. They pursue a rationale from the discipline of economics, which predicts that as the supply of a given resource dwindles, the price will rise. Then, one of two things, or both, will occur: Consumption will decrease, or because the resource is more valuable, greater efforts will be made to locate and process it and thus increase the supply.

The second presenter at the Symposium, Luis Camacho, Vice President of the University of Costa Rica, spoke about the First World/Third World controversy. Assuming there is a problem of world-wide overconsumption and a growing scarcity of resources, is it caused by excessive and unsustainable growth in developing countries, or is it the result of "hyperconsumption" in developed countries? A child born in the United States will consume 30 to 70 times more resources in a lifetime than a child born in an impoverished country. Predictably, developing countries believe that any scaling back should come in the developed countries. Developed countries, just as predictably, are loathe to do so, and they point to the greater population growth in developing countries as the true problem.

The third speaker was Father Thomas Berry, a self-styled "historian of cultures," whose work deals with humankind's proper role in the earth's ecosystem and the cosmos. He faulted business leaders for being too myopic, concentrating only on growth and profits, and using up the earth's resources at an ever faster rate only to create ever growing quantities of waste that the earth's ecosystem can no longer absorb. He advised that all institutions—the economy, government, schools, medicine, and religion—are mere subsystems of the universe. Thus, there can be no such thing as a healthy economy unless the earth's overall system is also healthy.

Overconsumption is not a new issue. Thirty years ago, before the first Arab oil embargo, it was common for electric utility companies to promote the sale of electric appliances. A billboard at Christmastime showed an electric blanket with a red ribbon tied around it. The more electric blankets that were sold, the more electricity the utility would sell. Another advertising campaign pictured an electric dishwasher with the caption, "Don't be a dishwasher, buy one!"

Now such promotion strategies are all but impossible. No utility company would encourage its customers to use (buy) more energy. In fact, utilities do just the opposite. Scarcely a month goes by that they do not include a flyer with their monthly bills that explains ways for customers to use *less* energy. This is a form of "demarketing." How extraordinary that a company would use traditional marketing tactics to try to reduce the consumption of its product.

Other examples of demarketing exist. The major breweries urge responsible consumption of alcoholic beverages. Current social constraints would not allow them to promote unlimited consumption of beer. State lotteries and casinos must be circumspect in promoting gambling because they do not want to be perceived as encouraging nongamblers to take it up. Clearly, these examples are exceptions to the normal function of marketing; most marketers work hard to encourage more consumers to buy more of their product more often.

Overconsumption and its adverse effects on the earth will not begin to have a serious effect until well into the future, yet futurists and ecologists warn that consumers should begin changing their habits now. It is not too early for marketers to become familiar with at least the outlines of the problem. A good place to start is a small book by Alan Durning (1992) titled *How Much Is Enough? The Consumer Society and the Future of the Earth*. Durning describes (p. 20) the issue as a true conundrum: "a problem admitting of no satisfactory solution."

If developing nations increased their per-capita consumption levels to those of the developed world, it would surely hasten the degradation of the earth's fragile life-support systems, Durning writes. Yet it is morally indefensible, he argues, to deny such advantages to the impoverished people of the world. Furthermore, it is probably impossible politically to reduce consumption in developed countries. So there is the stand-off.

Certainly, Durning is correct in describing this as a conundrum. Not only is there no apparent solution to the problem, but there is also little agreement as to how serious the problem is. Even so, it behooves marketers to become familiar with the arguments and to make certain they have a seat at the table when the debate begins in earnest.

Given that the heart and soul of marketing is increasing consumption, it is difficult to imagine a business world in which demarketing became the rule. But utilities and brewers have learned to live with their respective forms of holding back consumption. In time, other industries may need to create and practice other evolved forms of marketing that fulfill organizational goals and are more in harmony with the earth's systems.

1. What is overconsumption, and to what extent are marketers responsible for it?

2. There are no laws limiting the marketing of electricity, beer, or gambling. How do you explain the reluctance of marketers in those industries to promote their products aggressively?

References

Adams, Chris (2001), "FDA Tells Roche's U.S. Unit to Halt Ad for Weight Loss Drug," *The Wall Street Journal*, (May 18), B8.

Brown, Stephen, Pauline Maclaren, and Lorna Stevens (1996), "Marcadia Postponed: Marketing, Utopia, and the Millennium," *Journal of Marketing Management*, 12 (7), 671–83.

Cahill, Joseph B. (1998), "Credit Cards Invade a New Market Niche: The Mentally Disabled," *The Wall Street Journal*, (November 10), A1.

Daskou, Sofia (2000), "The Science of 'Relating': Consumers' Views of Market Relationships," paper presented at the International Conference on Business Economics, Marketing and Management, Athens, Greece (May).

Davidson, Kirk (1996), *Selling Sin: The Marketing of Socially Unacceptable Products*. Westport, CT: Quorum Press.

Durning, Alan (1992), *How Much Is Enough? The Consumer Society and the Future of the Earth*. New York: W.W. Norton & Company.

Hamilton, Joan (1998), "Taking on the Gene Tinkerers," *BusinessWeek*, (April 13), 14.

Irwin, Neil (2001), "Deal Raises Privacy Questions About Data," *The Washington Post*, (July 20), E1.

Lester, Toby (2001), "The Reinvention of Privacy," *Atlantic Monthly*, (March 27), (accessed May 21, 2002), [available at http://www.theatlantic.com/issues/2001/03/lester-p1.htm].

Nomani, Asra Q. (1998), "Naked Ambition: Tantra May Be Old, But It Has Generated a Hot Modern Market—Ancient Hindu Sex Practice Gets New-Age Makeover," *The Wall Street Journal*, (December 7), A1.

Ono, Yumiko (1998), "Where Are the Gloves? They Were Stocklifted by a Rival Producer," *The Wall Street Journal*, (May 15), A1.

Orwall, Bruce (2001), "Dinosaur Ad Invades Papers' Editorial Space," *The Wall Street Journal*, (July 18), B8.

Ottman, Jacquelyn (1996), "Suggestions for Environmental Labeling," *Marketing News*, 30 (June 3), 13.

Roberts, Paul Craig (1998), "Who Did More for Mankind, Mother Teresa or Mike Milken?" *BusinessWeek*, (March 2), 28.

Sandberg, Jared (1997), "Ply and Pry: How Business Pumps Kids on the Web," *The Wall Street Journal*, (June 9), B1.

Semon, Thomas (1996), "Can We Afford To Be Honest?" *Marketing News*, 30 (June 3), 5.

Swisher, Kara (2001), "Boom Town: Will the Internet Abandon Its Freedom to Avoid Controversies?—Battles Over Portals' Links to Adult Entertainment May Alter Web's Character," *The Wall Street Journal*, (April 23), B1.

Varney, Christine (2000), "The Death of Privacy," *Newsweek*, (Special Issue), (accessed May 21, 2002), [available at http://www.hhlaw.com/publications/pdf/VarneyNewsweek.pdf].

The Washington Post (1998), "Transformation, Cosmetic Surgery," advertising supplement, (April 24), 5, 10.

Weingarten, Gene (2001), "Why Not the Worst? We Promised To Find the Armpit of America," *The Washington Post*, (December 2), W12.

Yoxen, Edward (1983), *The Gene Business*. New York: Harper & Row.

Index

A

Abercrombie & Fitch, 147
Absentee ownership, 116
Absolute liability, 27
ACNielsen, 132
Adams, Chris, 95–96
Adidas, 157
Advanced Genetic Sciences, 151
Advertising, 77–108
  banner, 102
  Calvin Klein, 147, 170–72
  comparative, 164–65
  demeaning competitor's product in, 145
  direct-to-consumer, 96–97, 98
  dishonest, 77, 111
  distinction between editorial copy and, 103–4, 107
  explicit, 146
  false, 59
  fashion, 147, 154–56, 170–72
  infomercials as, 106–8
  manipulation in, 89–91
  marketing of hope in, 80–82
  negative, 163–64
  newspaper of *Jurassic Park III*, 102–5
  political, 163–65
  of prescription drugs, 95–98
  projection of images on products, 102
  puffery in, 77, 83–85, 148
  regulation of, 35
  sexual images in, 78, 146–47
  sponsorship as form of, 166–69
  taste in, 78–79
  trust in, 86–88
  unwanted, 131
  whole truth in, 78
Advocacy groups, 68, 174
African Americans
  marketing of alcohol to, 16
  marketing of cigarettes to, 15–16

Alcohol
  excessive student consumption of, 173–76
  marketing of, 16
  sale of beverages, 178–79
Aloe'ha Beverage Corp., 83
Amazon.com, 58–59, 128–29, 137
American Association of Advertising Agencies (AAAA), ethics code of, 84
American Express, 128, 164
American Telephone & Telegraph (AT&T), 37–38, 39
America Online (AOL), 178
Anheuser-Busch, 38, 174
Arby's, 19
Arrogance, legitimacy and, 95–98
Automated teller machine (ATM) fees, ethics of, 69–71
Avis, 135

B

Banana Republic, 38
Banking, ethics of automated teller machine fees, 69–71
Banner ads, 102
Bargaining, 60–62
Barnum, P. T., 82, 161
Berry, Thomas, xi, 186
Blockbuster Inc., 152
Bookstore Santa Cruz, 115–17
Bovine somatrotropin (BST), 152
Boycott, 47–48
Brand names, 73
Brands, identities of, 37–40
Bribes
  gifts as, 99–101
  nonprofits and, 167–68
Brown, Stephen, 8, 9
Budweiser, 19
Burke, Edmund, xii
Burroughs Wellcome, 74